365
Bible Stories
for
Children

DERRYDALE BOOKS
New York

This 1997 edition is published by DERRYDALE BOOKS, an imprint of Random
House Value Publishing, Inc., 201 E. 50th Street, New York, NY 10022.

DERRYDALE BOOKS is a trademark of Random House Value Publishing, Inc.

Random House

New York • Toronto • London • Sydney • Auckland
http://www.randomhouse.com/

Printed and bound in the United States of America.

Library of Congress Cataloging-in-Publication Data
    Burnette, Melanie M.
    365 Bible stories for children / Melanie M. Burnette.
        p.   cm.
    Summary: A retelling of popular stories from the Bible, one for each
day of the year.
    ISBN 0-517-18820-1
    1. Bible stories, English–Juvenile literature.   (1. Bible stories) I. Title
    BS551.2.B88   1997
    220.9'505–dc21   97-34904
                                                                          CIP
                                                                          AC

8 7 6 5 4 3 2 1

1. GOD MAKES
HEAVEN AND EARTH

Genesis 1 - 2

Before there was heaven and earth, there was only darkness. God said, "Let there be light!" And light appeared and filled the sky. Then God began to work on creating the earth. He commanded the rivers to lie in their banks and the oceans to roll back from the land. He made plants and trees to grow on the land and to bear fruit.

Above the land, God made the sun to give light by day and the moon and stars to twinkle by night. When everything was ready, God created living creatures to make the earth their home.

First God made the fish that swim in the water and the birds that fly in the air. On the next day, God made all the animals, big and small, to walk the earth.

God was very pleased with the world he had made. He looked down upon it and said, "It is good!"

2. GOD MAKES MAN AND WOMAN

Genesis 1 - 2

God wanted one more creature to make the world complete. This creature would be very special to God. God took clay from the earth and molded it into the shape of a man. When God breathed into the man, he came to life.

Then God named the man Adam, and took him to a beautiful place called the Garden of Eden. He put Adam to work naming all the animals, insects, birds, and fish.

There were many fruit trees in the garden. God told Adam that he could pick any of the fruit except the fruit from the tree of the knowledge of good and evil. "If you eat the fruit from that tree you will die," God said.

Although the garden was very lovely and Adam had much to do, he was still lonely. God knew this so he lay Adam down to sleep and took a rib from his side. From the rib God created a woman, Eve, to be with Adam. Together they walked in the garden, talking with God and doing his work. They were very happy living in the perfect world God had made.

3. ADAM AND EVE ARE TEMPTED

Genesis 3

Among the living things in the Garden of Eden was a snake. He crawled and hissed like the other snakes, but this snake was really God's enemy, Satan. He came to the garden to destroy all of the lovely things that God had made.

One day the snake asked Eve if God had told her not to eat the fruit from the trees.

"No," said Eve, "We can eat any fruit except the fruit of the tree of the knowledge of good and evil. God said if we eat that fruit we will die."

"You won't die," said the snake. "You will be wise like God if you eat that fruit."

Eve looked at the beautiful fruit, and she thought if she could just take one little bite then she would be wise like the snake said. So she picked a piece of the fruit. She bit into it then gave it to Adam so that he could have this wisdom also.

The wisdom Satan promised did not come. Adam and Eve had disobeyed God and they felt very bad. Later that evening, God called to them but they didn't answer. They went to hide among the trees where they picked leaves to cover their bodies.

God called, "Where are you, Adam?"

Adam and Eve walked very slowly out to meet God. They were afraid of him now because they knew they had done the one and only thing God had asked them not to do.

4. THE PUNISHMENT

Genesis 3

God was very sad when he saw Adam and Eve. When he asked Adam if they had eaten fruit from the forbidden tree, Adam blamed Eve.

"It was Eve who handed me the fruit," he said.

"I'm not to blame," said Eve. "The snake tricked me."

God explained to each of them that they could no longer live in the Garden of Eden because they had disobeyed him. Adam and Eve would have to go out into the world. They would have to work very hard to make crops grow. Weeds and thorns would grow up from the earth. The days would be long and tiring. And when they grew old, Adam and Eve would die and their bodies would return to the earth.

"You chose to disobey me," said God. "Now you must live apart from me."

Adam and Eve walked out of the Garden, and God sent angels with flaming swords to guard the entrance so they could not come back.

5. CAIN AND ABEL

Genesis 4

Once Adam and Eve had made a home away from the Garden of Eden, they had their first child, a boy named Cain. Soon afterward they had another son named Abel. The two boys grew up to be very different. Abel became a shepherd. He loved and trusted God and offered a lamb as a gift to God.

Cain was a farmer. He gave God a gift of corn he had grown in his fields. But Cain had much pride and stubborness inside him.

God knew what was in the heart of each brother. He accepted Abel's gift, but not Cain's. Cain became very angry with God and started to walk away from him.

"Why are you so angry?" God asked. "If you would only do what's right you would be happy."

Cain did not listen to God. Instead he became more angry at God and more jealous of his brother, Abel.

6. BROTHER KILLS BROTHER

Genesis 4

Cain knew Abel had pleased God in a way that he seemed unable to do. Cain grew more jealous of his brother every day. Finally, he made a plan to do away with his brother. He asked Abel to walk out to the fields with him.

Abel was glad that Cain wanted to be with him. He hoped they could love each other like real brothers again. His dream came to a bitter end when Cain raised his hand and hit Abel, killing him instantly. Cain walked away, leaving Abel's body in the field.

"Where's your brother, Cain?" Cain heard God's voice calling to him.

"How should I know?" Cain said. "It is not for me to look out for my brother all the time."

But God knew what had happened and spoke again to Cain. "Your brother's blood cries out to me! You must be punished for this evil thing, Cain. Leave this land, for it will no longer grow your crops. You will wander through this world in fear from now on."

Like his parents before him, Cain had disobeyed God and chosen a path that led him away from happiness.

7. NOAH LISTENS TO GOD

Genesis 6

For many years after Cain murdered his brother Abel, evil continued to spread throughout the earth. More and more people chose to displease God by living their lives apart from him. God tried to speak to the people in many different ways, but they would not listen.

Only one man seemed eager to do God's will. His name was Noah. God came to Noah one day and told him what must be done.

"There is so much evil in the world that I can no longer save it," God said. "I will send a flood so deep that everything living on earth will be destroyed. You must begin building a giant boat or ark so you and your family can survive."

Noah listened to God's instructions. The ark should have room for Noah and his wife as well as his three sons and their wives. Also, Noah must make space for two of every living creature God had created.

8. BUILDING THE ARK

Genesis 7

Noah started to work right away. He collected the wood and tar for the ark. He set aside smaller pieces of lumber to make pens for the animals. Many people passed by Noah's house while he worked and made jokes about him. Noah pleaded with the people to stop being bad and listen to God, but they walked away.

Almost one hundred years later, Noah finished the ark. Then he began to gather a male and a female from many of the animals. God wanted to be sure that new creatures would be born on the earth when the flood was over.

Noah and his family collected enough food to last many days and put it on the boat. Then God came to Noah and told him the time had come to load everyone up. A week later, the rain started to come down. It rained all day and all night for many days.

Water began to pour over the roads. It raced through people's houses, covering everything in its path. Many weeks passed and the water grew deeper until only Noah's ark was left floating on the water.

9. THE FLOOD ENDS

Genesis 8

Noah and his family stayed in the ark for nearly six months before the rain stopped. Slowly, the flood water went down until one day they felt the boat stop on solid ground. They were sitting on the mountains of Ararat, but they stayed in the boat because God had not told them it was safe to come out yet.

For six more weeks they waited. Finally, Noah set free a raven. It flew in circles around the boat. Then he sent a dove. It flew for a while, but came back to settle on the ark.

The next week, Noah let the dove out again. She flew off into the distance and came back carrying an olive branch. The next time Noah sent the dove out, she did not come back. That was a sign to Noah and his family that the land was dry enough to live on again.

God told Noah, "It is time to leave the boat now. The flood is gone."

10. THE RAINBOW

Genesis 9

Now Noah set all the animals, birds, and insects free. They hurried away to find new homes on the land. Everyone was happy to be out of the boat for they had been inside it nearly nine whole months.

Noah and his family built an altar so they could offer gifts to God and thank him for keeping them safe in the flood. God blessed them and told Noah and his sons, Shem, Ham, and

Japheth to go out and have many children. Then God made a promise to Noah. He said that no matter how badly people behave, he would never again destroy everything on earth.

"I will send you a sign so you will always remember my promise," God said. "When the rains come down, don't be afraid. Look up and see my rainbow with many beautiful colors. Then you will know you are safe."

11. THE TOWER OF BABEL

Genesis 11

Noah and his sons obeyed God's command to have many children. Soon the earth was populated again with lots of people. Some of the people were good and followed God's word. But there were some who wanted to gather in one place and build a city and a great tower to honor themselves.

God was very unhappy with these people because they were not following his plan for them.

The people who worked on the tower all spoke the same language as did everyone who lived on the earth during that time. God divided them into different groups and made them speak different languages. They could not understand one another, and they had to give up building their city and the great tower.

The people then scattered to other lands and their tower sat unfinished. They called it the Tower of Babel because 'babel' means 'mixed up,' just like the people who built it.

12. ABRAHAM FOLLOWS GOD

Genesis 11 - 12

A man called Abraham, who was a descendant of Noah's son Shem, lived in a big city where there was plenty of food and water for everyone. Abraham and his wife Sarah liked the many comforts of the city. They worked alongside their neighbors, but they did not worship with them. Abraham believed in God. He did not go to the temples to worship idols like the others did.

God spoke to Abraham one day. God told him to take Sarah and his nephew Lot and leave the city for a new land.

"This land is called Canaan," God said. "I will bless you and give you this country and it will belong to you and your family."

Abraham trusted God. He knew the trip would be long and hard. They would have to leave most of their possessions behind in order to make the journey. But Abraham gathered together what they could pack on the donkeys and set out for Canaan. He trusted God.

13. LOT'S CHOICE

Genesis 13

A braham, Sarah, Lot, and their many servants traveled very far to reach the land of Canaan. Once they reached it, Abraham and Lot began to let their many cattle and sheep graze on the green fields. Soon their herds were so big that the servants who cared for the animals began to argue with one another over the water supply in the well.

11

"This is a very big country," Abraham said to Lot one day. "We should divide our flocks and use separate areas so there will be plenty of water and land for us both."

God had given Canaan to Abraham so he could have taken first choice and picked the best place to settle. But Abraham was not selfish. He let Lot choose first.

Lot was not generous like Abraham. He picked the best land down near the river Jordan. Abraham said good-bye to Lot and walked off in the opposite direction. He could have been angry at Lot, but Abraham knew that God would do as he promised. Abraham thanked God and praised him for bringing them to the Promised Land.

14. GOD'S PROMISE TO ABRAHAM

Genesis 14 - 15

Soon after Lot settled in the city of Sodom near the Jordan River, a war broke out. Lot was taken prisoner along with some other people of the city. Abraham heard about Lot's troubles and hurried to his rescue.

The chiefs of Sodom thanked Abraham and offered him a reward. Abraham did not want their riches. He wanted something that was much more important. Sarah and Abraham had never been able to have any children. Now Abraham was afraid they were too old.

That night God called to Abraham to come out of his tent. "Look at the stars in the sky," God told Abraham. "I promise that you will one day have as many children and grandchildren as there are stars. They will walk this earth and call this country their own."

God told Abraham that he and Sarah would soon have a son. Even though it didn't seem possible, Abraham had faith that God would keep his promise.

15. HAGAR, THE SERVANT GIRL

Genesis 16

Many years went by after God made the promise to Abraham and still no child had been born. Sarah began to doubt that the promise would come true. She had a servant girl named Hagar. In those days a wife could give her servant to her husband as a second wife. If Abraham and Hagar had a child, it would become Abraham's heir.

Abraham went along with the plan to please Sarah. But when Hagar did become pregnant with a child, she was so thrilled that Sarah did not want to be around her anymore. Sarah was mean to Hagar, and Hagar finally had to run away.

It was not God's plan for Hagar to have Abraham's baby. The promise was that Abraham and Sarah would have a child of their own. Still God took pity on Hagar.

"Go back to your mistress, Hagar," God said. "I will keep you safe."

Hagar listened to God and did what he told her. Soon she gave birth to a son and named him Ishmael.

16. THREE VISITORS

Genesis 17 - 18

God spoke to Abraham again after Ishmael was born. He reminded him of the covenant, the special agreement, that he and Abraham had.

"I will bless your child," God told Abraham.

Abraham thought God meant his child Ishmael. But God told him again that Sarah would have their baby, a boy they would name Isaac.

As he sat at the door of his tent one day, thinking of the many things God had told him, Abraham saw three men walking toward him. Abraham welcomed the men and invited them to stay for dinner. The men agreed, for they were very tired and hungry. They all sat down to a meal of fresh-baked bread and tender meat.

One of the men said to Abraham, "By next year, Sarah will have the son you have been promised."

Abraham was shocked. How could the visitor know such things? Sarah heard the man also. She thought he was making a joke and laughed out loud.

"Why did Sarah laugh?" asked the man. "The Lord can do anything, even the impossible."

"I didn't laugh," said Sarah. She was embarrassed.

Abraham suddenly understood what was happening. The man who spoke was really God himself. He only disguised himself as a man so he could come to Abraham and tell him that the promise would come true very soon.

17. A WARNING TO LOT

Genesis 18 – 19

Soon it was time for the visitors to go on their way. Abraham walked with them toward the city of Sodom. God began to tell Abraham what he was planning to do.

"The people of Sodom and Gomorrah are very bad people," God said. "They have turned away from me and I am going to destroy the cities."

Abraham was afraid because Lot and his family still lived in Sodom.

But God had sent his angels ahead to warn Lot and his family. The angels found Lot at the city gates. They told him that God was planning to destroy the city and he must get out quickly.

Lot went home to tell his family. His wife and daughters began packing their things, but they were taking their time. The angels grabbed their arms and hurried them onto the road.

"Run, run, and don't look back," cried the angels.

Lot and his family ran toward the hills. They tried to keep their eyes on the road ahead of them. Suddenly, Lot's wife could stand it no longer. She turned around to look at Sodom and when she did she became a pillar of salt.

18. SODOM IS DESTROYED

Genesis 19

Lot and his daughters kept on running. The sky behind them was turning red. As the sun began to rise over

Sodom, God sent fire down on the city. Everything in Sodom and Gomorrah was set ablaze and destroyed.

The whole sky looked as if it were on fire. Lot was thankful that he had obeyed God. He took his daughters up into the mountains to live in a cave where they would be safe.

Abraham saw the smoke and fire from his tent, and he knew that God had carried out his plan. He was very sad on that day. God had not turned his back on him, though. Abraham would soon have a son and later he would have many grandchildren and great-grandchildren who would come to be known as the Jews. They would live in God's Promised Land, called Israel.

19. THE BIRTH OF ISAAC

Genesis 21

Almost a year later, Sarah gave birth to her promised son. Abraham named the boy Isaac just as God had told him to. He understood why God had chosen that name. Isaac means 'laughter,' and when the baby was born there was much laughter and joy in Abraham's house.

Sarah loved her son very much and was very protective of him. When Isaac was a little older, he liked playing outside. Ishmael, Isaac's half-brother, was a lot older than him. He liked to play rougher games than little Isaac.

One day Ishmael began to tease Isaac. Sarah saw what happened and was angry. She went to tell Abraham. Sarah insisted that Ishmael and his mother, Hagar, be sent away. That bothered Abraham because Ishmael was also his son. He didn't want him to go away.

"Don't worry about your son, Ishmael," God said to Abraham. "I will care for him and his mother. Ishmael will grow to lead a great nation of his own."

So Abraham agreed with Sarah's plan.

20. GOD'S PLAN FOR ISHMAEL

Genesis 21

Abraham had given Hagar and Ishmael some food and water for their trip. They walked for many miles and soon their supplies ran out. There was nothing but sand all around them. They became very thirsty and weak.

Hagar left her son lying beside a little bush. She walked a little farther and sat down with her back to the burning sun.

"Don't be afraid," God said to her. "Go and comfort your son."

Hagar looked up to see a well very close by. She ran and brought water from it to Ishmael. Soon they were both strong enough to go on.

Ishmael and Hagar made their home in a place called Paran. It was close to the country of Egypt. When Ishmael grew up, he married an Egyptian girl and they had many heirs.

As God had promised, the children of Ishmael later formed a mighty nation and called themselves Arabs. Throughout all of history the Arabs and Isaac's people, the Jews, have fought with one another just like Ishmael and Isaac did as children.

21. A TEST OF FAITH

Genesis 22

Abraham and Sarah rejoiced in their son, Isaac. Their love for him grew more and more each day. Abraham was very thankful to God.

God knew that Abraham was a faithful person. Still, there was one more test to show Abraham that God was different from any other gods. God asked Abraham to bring Isaac to a nearby mountain and offer him as a sacrifice.

Abraham was very troubled, yet he had always trusted in God before. He believed in God's plan for Isaac, so the next morning he took the boy to the mountain as God had asked.

Isaac helped his father lay the stones for the altar. When it was done, Isaac asked where was the lamb for the sacrifice. Abraham answered, "The Lord will provide that." Then he lifted Isaac onto the altar and took out a knife. Abraham lifted the knife in the air. Just then he heard God calling to him.

"Don't hurt your son, Abraham," God said. "You have proved that you truly believe in me by your faith."

Abraham lifted his son from the altar. In the nearby brush he spotted a ram. Abraham killed it and laid it on the altar to be burned as an offering to God to thank him for sparing Isaac.

22. THE SEARCH FOR A WIFE

Genesis 24

Sarah had grown very old. She lived long enough to see Isaac reach manhood before she passed away. Shortly afterwards, Abraham decided it was time for Isaac to take a wife.

There were many beautiful women in Canaan, but Abraham didn't want Isaac to marry one of them. He wanted to find a woman from his native land who loved and worshipped God as Abraham and Isaac did.

Abraham sent a servant to find a suitable young woman and bring her back.

"The woman may not be willing to make such a long journey," said the servant. "Would I then bring Isaac to her?"

Abraham refused. He knew it was God's plan for Isaac to stay there in the Promised Land and build a great nation.

"If the woman won't come back with you, I will release you from your promise," Abraham told the servant.

The servant left the next day. He took ten camels and loaded them with lots of gifts and supplies.

23. A WOMAN NAMED REBEKAH

Genesis 24

On the way back to Abraham's homeland, the servant prayed to God and asked for help to find the right woman. By the time he reached the town, he had a plan.

Many young women were gathered at the well as he entered the town. They offered water to travelers as a gesture of kindness. "If one of these women offers to get water for my camels also, I will know she is God's chosen one."

About that time, a beautiful young woman walked up to where the servant was kneeling.

"May I have some water?" asked the servant. The woman offered her water jar to him.

"Do your camels need water, too?" she said, dipping the jar in the well again. She filled a trough with plenty of water for the animals.

The servant knew he had found the woman that Isaac would marry. When he asked her name, she told him she was Rebekah and that she was from Nahor's family. The servant rejoiced because Nahor was Abraham's brother. He gave Rebekah some of the gifts he had brought and asked if they could go meet her father. He wanted to ask permission to take Rebekah back to marry Isaac.

24. ISAAC MARRIES REBEKAH

Genesis 24

Rebekah's family was happy to greet the servant when they heard he was sent by Abraham. He told them how he had prayed to God to find the right bride for Isaac. He told them of his plan, and how Rebekah had come to him.

"I would like to take Rebekah back with me right away," said the servant.

The family agreed that the marriage would be a good one. They helped her to pack her things. The servant gave the family many gifts he had brought with him on his camels. Then he thanked God for leading him to Rebekah.

They set off the next morning on the long journey. It was many days before they reached Canaan. As they entered Abraham's fields, they saw a young man walking towards them. That was the first time Isaac and Rebekah had ever seen one another. But they knew from the very beginning that they were meant to be together.

God blessed the marriage of Isaac and Rebekah as he promised Abraham he would. Isaac loved Rebekah very much and took good care of her. But it was many more years before God fulfilled his promise that Isaac and Rebekah would bear grandchildren for Abraham.

25. THE TWINS

Genesis 25

Isaac was very surprised one day to find out that Rebekah would have twins! According to the law, the firstborn son was to receive most of his father's land and money.

Isaac and Rebekah named the first twin Esau and the second, Jacob. Although they were twins, Esau and Jacob were not very much alike at all. The older brother liked to hunt in the woods and killed many deer. When he brought them home, his brother Jacob would cook a delicious stew using the meat.

Esau came in from hunting one day. He had not eaten all day and was very, very hungry.

"Let me have some of that stew," he said to Jacob.

Jacob wanted to be head of the family one day and have all its riches. He said to Esau, "I'll give you something to eat if you'll give me your birthright in return."

Esau was more concerned about being hungry than about something that would happen many years in the future.

"Yes, you can have it," said Esau. "If you don't feed me now, I'll starve anyway."

Jacob handed Esau the bowl of stew and he ate until he was satisfied.

26. THE TRICK

Genesis 27

The day soon came for Isaac to give his blessing to the first-born son. He called to his son Esau and asked him to kill a deer and fix him a special stew.

"I must give you my blessing soon" said Isaac, for I am very old and I will not live much longer."

Rebekah heard what Isaac said. She remembered God had told her that her younger son would lead the family. That meant Jacob must be the one to receive Isaac's blessing. She ran to find Jacob.

"Kill two goats for me to cook," she told him. "I will make a good stew. Your father's eyesight is very bad. He will think you are Esau and give you the blessing."

Jacob did not like this plan. He looked nothing like his brother. Esau had hair on his arms and chest.

But Rebekah fixed the stew and brought some of Esau's clothes for Jacob to put on. She tied skins from the goats they had killed around Jacob's hands.

"Here is your stew, father," Jacob said.

Isaac took the bowl from him. "You sound like Jacob," he said. Then Isaac touched his son and felt the goat skin on his hands. They felt hairy like Esau's, so Isaac settled back and began to eat the stew.

27. ESAU'S DISCOVERY

Genesis 27

The stew that Rebekah had fixed for Isaac tasted so good, Isaac ate every bit. When he was done, he touched Jacob's head and blessed him with the blessing he meant for Esau. Jacob left and hurried away to hide.

Not long after that, Esau returned from hunting. When Esau walked into his father's tent, Isaac knew right away he had been fooled by Jacob. He had given the birthright and the special blessing to the wrong son.

Esau yelled aloud, "As soon as our father dies, I will find Jacob and kill him."

Rebekah heard this. She was very frightened. She knew Jacob had to get away from his brother.

Jacob had not yet married, so Rebekah told Isaac that Jacob should go back to her homeland to find a bride. Isaac knew it would be better for his son to marry a woman who believed in God. Esau had married two women from Canaan. They worshipped idols made of stone. This made Isaac sad because he loved God. He told Rebekah to send Jacob on his way.

28. GOD SPEAKS TO JACOB

Genesis 28

Jacob set out for Haran, the land of his mother's people. It was not a happy journey because Jacob had done many bad things to hurt his brother, and he was very sorry.

He found a piece of stone flat enough to use as a pillow, so he lay down to sleep for the night. Jacob began to dream of stairs that reached up into heaven. He could see angels walking up and down the stairs. A voice called out to him, and he saw God standing next to him.

"I am the God of Abraham and Isaac," God said. "I made a promise to them that I will now make to you. You will return to this land one day, and you will have many children who will live over all the earth."

God promised Jacob that he would always be with him and care for him. Jacob woke up feeling full of God's love. To thank God, Jacob built an altar using the stone where he'd laid his head. Then he prayed to God and promised that if God would truly look after him and bring him home, Jacob would serve God always.

Jacob called the place Bethel because it means "house of God." He left the rocks piled there to remind him of the promises he and God had spoken to each other.

29. THE TWO SISTERS

Genesis 29

Jacob continued his journey until he came to the well at the entrance to Haran, his mother's homeland. He asked the people there if they knew Laban, who was Jacob's uncle.

"That is his daughter," they said, pointing to a girl coming towards them.

Jacob helped her to water her flock of sheep. She told him her name was Rachel and took him home to meet her father. Laban invited Jacob to stay at his house and help him tend his sheep. He offered to pay Jacob fair wages for his work. After Jacob got to know Rachel, he knew what he wanted.

"I will work for you for seven years," he told Laban, "If you will let me marry your daughter, Rachel."

Laban agreed to the marriage, and Jacob worked hard for seven years.

The wedding feast took place as planned. That night Laban took the bride to Jacob's tent. It was so dark Jacob could not see his bride. In the light of the dawn, Jacob discovered that he had actually married Rachel's sister, Leah. Laban had tricked Jacob into marrying her because she was the oldest.

"You can marry Rachel, also," Laban told Jacob. "But you will have to stay and work for me another seven years."

Jacob felt he had no choice. He loved Rachel very much. He cared for both sisters along with their servant girls, and soon they began to bear him children.

30. JACOB'S RETURN

Genesis 30 – 31

Rachel was the last of Jacob's wives to have a child, a baby boy named Joseph. Jacob finally had everything he wanted. One day he told Laban he planned to go back to his home.

Laban did not want Jacob to leave. He offered to start paying him for his work. Jacob told him he would stay only if Laban gave him a flock of sheep and goats.

Jacob was a good shepherd. His flocks and herds began to grow. Although Laban also grew richer from Jacob's work, he and his sons resented Jacob. They tried to think of ways to cheat Jacob.

God was true to the promise made to Jacob at Bethel. God

looked after Jacob and all his family and told Jacob it was time to return to Canaan. The next day, Jacob and his family left on their journey without telling Laban they were going.

When Laban found out they were gone, he followed after them. He soon joined up with them, but only to tell his daughters and their children good-bye. Laban told Jacob to go on his way and he would not bother them anymore.

31. JACOB REACHES CANAAN

Genesis 32

Jacob wanted to return home, but he dreaded to see his brother, Esau. Esau had vowed to kill him after their father Isaac died, but Isaac was still alive. Jacob decided to send two messengers ahead to tell Esau that he wanted to make peace with him.

The messengers returned to Jacob with the news that Esau was coming to meet him with 400 soldiers. Jacob became very frightened. He prayed to God for help. He sent many gifts to Esau, then took his family across the Jordan River to be safe.

That night Jacob was alone. Someone came out of the darkness and attacked him. They wrestled through the night. Finally, the stranger touched Jacob's hip, knocking it out of joint. Jacob was hurt but he would not stop wrestling.

"What is your name?" asked the stranger.

"My name is Jacob."

"I'm going to change your name," the stranger said. "You will be called Israel for the one who has fought with God and with man and prevailed."

The stranger blessed Jacob and went on his way. Jacob was thankful. He had been face to face with God, and God had spared his life.

32. BROTHERS MEET AGAIN

Genesis 33

Jacob gathered his family together the next day, and they went out to meet Esau. Jacob walked in front. He wanted to be the first to greet his brother. If Esau still wanted to kill him, maybe he would go ahead and do it and leave his family alone.

At last Jacob was face to face with Esau. He bowed to him seven times. Esau ran towards him, throwing his arms around him. Jacob hugged him back. He was happy to be friends with his brother again.

Esau asked about the people with Jacob.

"These are the children God has blessed me with," said Jacob. He brought out the servants and their children first. Then he introduced Leah and Rachel to his brother.

"What were all those other animals that came before you?" he asked.

Jacob explained that he had many sheep and goats in his herds. He wanted to share them with his brother. Esau thanked Jacob and asked him if he could continue on with them on their journey. Jacob told him to go ahead since they could not travel as fast as Esau's group. Again Jacob felt blessed because God had helped him make peace with his brother.

33. RACHEL DIES

Genesis 35

God called upon Jacob to go to Bethel. Jacob knew right away where God meant for him to go. Bethel was the place where God had promised him that he would one day come back to the Promised Land. God had taken care of Jacob just like he said he would.

When they got to Bethel, Jacob and the others built an altar. Jacob poured oil over it to thank God for all that God had done. Once again, God came to speak with him on the pillar of stone. God talked to him again about the nation his children would become. Afterwards, Jacob and his family continued their journey.

Rachel was carrying her second child and she was very weary. When the baby was born, Rachel became sick and died. Jacob named the baby boy Benjamin. Then he put up a special stone to mark Rachel's grave. Jacob missed Rachel very much after she died.

34. THE FAVORITE SON

Genesis 37

Jacob had twelve sons, but he favored Joseph, Rachel's first-born. He showed his love for Joseph in many ways. Once he gave him a beautiful coat made up of many colors.

Joseph's brothers were jealous of him. The more special treatment he got, the more they hated him. Joseph had told them stories of a dream he had one night. He said they were out in the fields, harvesting the grain. The crops were bundled up in sheaves, and the brothers' sheaves began to bow to Joseph's sheaves. That really made the brothers angry.

"Do you now think you will reign over us?" they asked.

But Joseph had another dream. In it, he dreamed that the sun, moon, and eleven stars all bowed to him. His father heard about this dream and was very troubled by it.

"Does this mean that I and my wife and all your brothers must bow down before you?"

35. JOSEPH IN THE WELL

Genesis 37

Joseph's brothers had gone out into the fields to feed Jacob's animals. They had been gone for some time, and Jacob asked Joseph to go find them. The brothers saw Joseph coming toward them.

"Here comes Joseph the dreamer," they said. "Let's kill him and throw him in a pit. We can say a beast ate him up. No one will ever know. We'll see what happens to his big dreams then."

Reuben was Joseph's oldest brother. He knew it was wrong to kill the boy. He thought of a way to keep Joseph safe from the others.

"We shouldn't kill him," he said. "Let's just drop him down that dried-up well and scare him."

Joseph came closer. He was wearing the beautiful coat his father had given him. The brothers grabbed him and ripped it off. They dropped Joseph down into the dark well.

The brothers did not feel bad about harming their little brother. They sat down with their lunches and began to eat as if nothing had happened.

36. JOSEPH IS SOLD

Genesis 37

The brothers noticed a group of camels in the distance. When the caravan got closer, they could tell it was a group of traders on their way to Egypt. Judah leaned over to his brothers and asked them, "What good is it to kill Joseph and hide his body? Wouldn't it be better to sell him to these men?"

The brothers agreed. They dragged Joseph out of the pit and sold him as a slave for twenty silver pieces.

Reuben was not with the others. It was too late to save Joseph when he got back, though.

"What will we tell our father now?" asked Reuben.

One of the brothers picked up Joseph's coat of many colors. They poured goat's blood over it to make it look like Joseph had been attacked and killed by a wild beast. When they showed the coat to Jacob, he knew that his favorite son must be dead.

"I will mourn for him until I, too, am dead," he said. Jacob wept for his son, Joseph, and the other children could do nothing to comfort him.

37. JOSEPH PUT IN PRISON

Genesis 39

Joseph was sold to a man in Egypt named Potiphar. He was head of the guards who protected the Pharaoh, the king of Egypt. Joseph's master came to trust and like him very much because Joseph was a hard worker.

Potiphar's wife became very fond of Joseph, too. She started to follow him around the house as he did his chores. She tried to hug him and get him to come into her bedroom with her.

Joseph struggled to get away from her. He knew it was wrong to make love with another man's wife. That made the woman very angry. She lied to her husband about what had happened to make it look like Joseph had chased after her.

Potiphar believed his wife's tale and had Joseph put into prison. Even though he was locked away for something he didn't do, Joseph didn't turn away from God. And God stayed by Joseph's side through everything that happened to him.

38. DREAMS

Genesis 40

Joseph became the favorite of the jailer. He gave Joseph the job of looking after the other prisoners.

Two new prisoners arrived one day. One was the king's baker and the other was one of his butlers. The jailer told Joseph to take special care of these two, so every morning he came to their cell to make sure they were all right.

One morning they told Joseph they had both had strange dreams the night before.

"God knows what your dreams mean," Joseph said to them. "If you tell them to me, I can help you."

The butler, who was in charge of serving the king his wine, had dreamed of pressing grapes into the king's cup. Joseph told him that meant that he would be set free to go back to his job.

The baker told of three white baskets full of bread. He dreamed that birds flew down and ate the bread before he could give it to the Pharaoh.

"Three days from now, the king will order you to be killed," Joseph told the baker.

A birthday feast was held for the king three days later. He ordered the butler to go back to work but the baker was ordered to die, just as Joseph had told them.

39. JOSEPH GOES FREE

Genesis 41

Joseph stayed in prison for two more years after the butler was set free. Then the Pharaoh awoke one night from a very mysterious dream. He gathered the wisest men of the country together, but no one could tell him what the dream meant.

When the butler heard of the king's problem, he remembered the dream he had had in prison.

"Sir, I knew a man in prison who told me what my dreams meant," said the butler. "Everything he told me came true."

The king had Joseph brought before him. "Is it true that you can tell me what my dreams mean?" asked the king.

"I can't do it myself," said Joseph, "but God will help me."

The king told Joseph he had dreamed that he saw seven fat cows standing near the river. Seven skinny cows came by and ate the fat ones. Then he saw seven ripe ears of corn on a stalk. Seven sickly ears began to grow on the same stalk and ate up the good ears.

"God is warning you about a great famine," said Joseph. "Seven years of good crops will be followed by seven years when the crops won't grow, and your people will go hungry."

40. JOSEPH'S PLAN

Genesis 41

The king was very upset by what Joseph had told him. He did not want the people of Egypt to starve during the seven years of famine.

"If the king will do these things," said Joseph, "then the people can be saved."

Pharaoh listened closely to what Joseph told him.

"You must first find a wise man to be in charge of the crops during the seven good years. He can see that plenty of food is stored away. Then when the bad times come, he can see that the people get plenty to eat."

"No one could be better for that job than you," the king said to Joseph. "After all, you are the one God chose to bring us this message."

Joseph went to work for Pharaoh. He spent the first seven years travelling around the countryside in his chariot, making sure the grain was harvested and put away in the King's storehouses. The next seven years brought a great famine as Joseph had said. The people of Egypt cried out to their king for help.

"Go see Joseph," the king told them. "And do whatever he tells you."

41. HELP FOR THE BROTHERS

Genesis 42

Jacob, Joseph's father, heard of the great stores of grain in Egypt. He sent Joseph's brothers to buy some of it for their family. They made the long journey from Canaan to Egypt. When they got there, they were told that the governor of the city was in charge of the grain.

"We have come from Canaan to buy food for our families," they said.

"No, you have come only as spies to see how bad things are in Egypt," Joseph said.

"That is not true!" they said. "We are brothers. There were twelve of us, but one is gone and the other is with our father."

Benjamin was not with the brothers, so Joseph knew he was the one left behind. He told the others he would keep them prisoner and send one of them back to fetch the younger brother.

"That will prove to me that you aren't spies," he said.

42. SEND BENJAMIN

Genesis 42

The brothers stayed in prison for three days. Joseph came to speak with them again. This time he had another plan.

"Let one of your brothers stay here," he said. "The rest of you carry corn back to your home. But if you want to be safe, bring the younger brother back to me so I'll know you are really telling the truth.

They began to talk to each other in their native language, thinking that Joseph would not be able to understand them.

"It is a terrible thing that we did to our brother Joseph. Now we are being punished for it," they said.

Reuben said to them, "Didn't I tell you that we should not hurt the boy? You didn't listen to me and now we must pay for what we've done to him."

Joseph turned his back and wept when he heard what his brothers said about him. Then he sent all but his brother Simeon back to Canaan.

43. BACK TO EGYPT

Genesis 43

The food the brothers had brought back with them did not last long. The famine grew worse and Jacob told his sons they must go back to Egypt to buy more.

"We have already told you," said Judah. "The governor will not let us come back to the city unless we bring Benjamin."

Judah promised to take care of Benjamin and guard him with his life, so Jacob finally gave in. Joseph had returned the money that the brothers had brought to pay for the grain the last time, and Jacob told them they must take extra money to pay him back.

When the brothers reached Joseph's house, he invited them in for a meal.

"Is this the brother you call Benjamin?" he asked.

Benjamin walked toward his brother, but Joseph had to leave the room because he was so overcome with joy at the sight of his little brother.

Joseph made the brothers sit in a row according to their ages, and they were surprised by that. Then he sent food to their table, but Joseph made sure Benjamin's plate had the most of all.

44. THE SILVER CUP

Genesis 44

The next morning, Joseph ordered the brothers' sacks to be filled with grain for their journey home. Once again he returned all their money to them. But this time, Joseph asked the servants to do something unusual.

"Put my silver cup in the sack of the youngest brother," he told them.

After the brothers had journeyed outside the city, Joseph sent a servant to go after them.

"Which one of you has stolen my master's cup?" shouted the servant when he had reached them.

"We have taken nothing," they said. "Look, we have even returned the money that was sent back in our sacks. If you find one of us has the cup, kill him and take the rest of us as slaves."

"I will take the guilty one with me," said the servant. "The rest will go free."

The servant searched all the sacks. He saved Benjamin's for last because he was the youngest. He reached deep into the sack and there was the silver cup!

45. TOGETHER AGAIN

Genesis 45

Benjamin's brothers returned to the city with him. Judah fell down before Joseph and begged his forgiveness.

"Our father will die if we don't bring Benjamin back," he said. "Send him and keep me instead."

Judah continued to plead with Joseph until Joseph could stand it no longer. He sent the servants out of the room, then he spoke to his brothers in their native language.

"I am Joseph," he cried. "I am the brother you sold as a slave."

Joseph told his brothers not to feel guilty about what they had done to him. "God sent me here to help people stay alive during the famine. It will last five more years, but I will care for you and make sure you do not go hungry."

The Pharaoh told Joseph to send word for all his family to come to Egypt and settle there. Joseph sent his brothers back to Canaan loaded with gifts. He couldn't wait for them to tell his father the good news.

46. LEAVING CANAAN

Genesis 46 – 50

Jacob almost fainted when he heard that Joseph was alive. He wanted to see his son again very much, but he wasn't sure he should leave his homeland and move to Egypt. God told Jacob that he would be with him in Egypt and bring him back to Canaan when he died, so the family packed up and went on their way.

Jacob sent Judah on ahead to let Joseph know they would soon arrive in Egypt. Joseph was so excited, he went out to meet them where they had set up camp in a place called Goshen.

The reunion of Jacob and Joseph was a very happy one. Jacob said to his son, "I can die a happy man now because I have seen my son again."

Joseph asked five of his brothers to return with him to Egypt. They came before the king to ask him if they might stay in Goshen to tend their flocks because the land was very good there. Pharaoh was pleased to grant their request.

Jacob lived to be nearly 150 years old. Before he died, he called all of Joseph's children to his side and blessed them. Then the brothers took him back to Canaan to be buried.

47. THE ISRAELITES BECOME SLAVES

Exodus 1

Joseph died many years after his father, but his children had many children. The Egyptians began to be afraid because there were so many of Jacob's descendants—or Israelites as they were called.

A new pharaoh came into power. He didn't know what Joseph had done to save the Egyptian people in the great famine. He didn't like the Israelites because they were foreigners and he feared they would gain too much power.

Pharaoh put all the Israelites to work building huge buildings in the city. He treated them as slaves, but God was looking after his people as he had promised. In spite of the king's cruelty, their numbers grew.

Something more must be done to stop the Israelites, the king thought. The king called all the midwives (women who helped deliver babies) together and spoke to them.

"If you go to the house of an Israelite and a son is born, you must be sure that he dies."

The midwives were good women who feared God. They told the king that the Israelite women did not need their help.

Then the king became very angry. He told the people that every baby boy born to the Israelites must be found and thrown into the Nile River.

48. A BABY IS SAVED

Exodus 2

Not long after the king put his cruel law into effect, a baby boy was born to the family of Levi. The mother could not bear to see her baby hurt so she hid him for as long as she could. As the baby grew older, his mother planned how to save her child. She made a small boat from reeds and tar. She laid her baby in it and sent the baby's sister, Miriam, with him down to the river. Miriam set the little boat afloat and sat down in the bushes to watch.

Nearby, a group of women had come down to the water to bathe. One of these women was the Pharaoh's daughter. She saw the boat floating along and sent one of her servants after it.

"This must be an Israelite child," said the princess. The little boy began to cry so she picked him up and held him.

Then Miriam walked out of the bushes to speak to the princess. "Would you like one of the women to nurse the child till he is older?" she asked.

The princess agreed, and Miriam ran to get her mother.

"Take this baby home and nurse him until he is older," the princess said to the baby's mother. "Then I will take him to live with me."

The princess decided to call the baby Moses because he came from out of the water.

49. MOSES, THE PRINCE

Exodus 2

Moses grew up among the riches of the Egyptian Pharaoh. He knew that although he lived in the king's palace, he was an Israelite and he had pity on his people. The king was still treating them very badly.

One day, Moses rode out into the city in his chariot. He saw an Egyptian beating one of the Israelite slaves. Moses looked around but could see no one nearby. Then he attacked the Egyptian himself and killed him.

The next day, Moses saw two Israelites fighting each other.

"Why are you fighting with your brother?" he asked one man.

"Who are you to ask that?" he said. "What are you going to do? Kill me like you did that Egyptian yesterday?"

Moses' secret was no longer safe. If the king were to catch him now, he would be killed. So Moses fled to a nearby land called Midian. He was sitting by a well when seven sisters came to fetch some water.

Just then, a group of shepherds walked up and pushed the girls out of the way so they could get water first. Moses jumped up to help the girls. They were very grateful and told their father about the man who had helped them at the well. He asked Moses to come stay with them.

Moses became a shepherd for the father. He stayed with the family and eventually married one of the sisters.

50. THE BURNING BUSH

Exodus 3

Moses liked going out into the fields to look after his father-in-law's sheep. One day he took them to graze on the tender grass at the bottom of Mount Sinai. There he saw a bush that was covered with flames.

Moses looked closer at the bush. The flames burned hot but the bush was not burning! A voice began to speak to him from out of the fire.

"Moses!" the voice said. "I am the God of Abraham, Isaac and Jacob."

Moses hid his face for he was very much afraid.

"I know the terrible things that are happening to my people in Egypt," God said. "I have come to save them. You will lead my people back to the Promised Land of Canaan, Moses."

"I am not strong and wise enough to do such a thing," said Moses.

"Certainly, I will be with you," God said.

"But how will they know that?" asked Moses.

God told Moses to take the stick he was holding and throw it on the ground. When he did, the stick turned into a snake.

"Pick it up by its tail," God told Moses.

He did, and the snake turned back into a stick.

"I will give you the power to show these and other signs to the people so they will know I have sent you," God said.

51. MOSES AND THE PHARAOH

Exodus 4 - 5

On the way to Egypt, Moses met his brother Aaron and told him about all the things God had said. They went first to the Israelite leaders to give them God's message.

The people of Israel were very thankful that the Lord had sent someone to help them. They bowed down before Moses and Aaron and prayed to God. Then Moses and Aaron went to meet with the Pharaoh.

"The Lord God of Israel has told us that you must let his people go free," they said to the king.

"Who is this God?" the king asked. "I don't know him and I'm not about to free any of the Israelites."

He ordered Moses and Aaron out of the palace. Then Pharaoh ordered his men to stop bringing straw to the Israelite slaves for their bricks. "Make them go get their own," he said.

The Israelites now had twice as much work to do. They came to the Pharaoh to ask for mercy, but he would not help them. On the way back from the palace, they complained to Aaron and Moses about having to work harder then ever.

Moses spoke to the Lord. "Why have you sent me?" he asked. "I have done nothing but harm to these people."

God told Moses not to be impatient. "Just wait and see what I have in store for the Pharaoh."

52. DISASTER STRIKES EGYPT

Exodus 7 - 9

God sent Moses and Aaron again to warn Pharaoh that he must let the people of Israel go free. Aaron threw down the long stick which Moses had brought with him and it turned into a snake. The king ordered his sorcerers to throw down their rods as well. All the rods turned into snakes, but Aaron's snake swallowed them.

The miracle only made the king more stubborn. He refused again to let the Israelites leave. Again God spoke to Moses: "Tell Aaron to wave his rod over the rivers of Egypt." He did, and the rivers turned to blood.

The king's sorcerers could do nothing to change the water back. Then the Lord sent frogs jumping out of the nasty water. They covered the city. Pharaoh called for Moses and Aaron and promised to do as they asked if they would get rid of the frogs. The next day all the frogs were dead. When Pharaoh saw that he refused to let the people go.

This time God commanded Aaron to wave the stick over the earth. Tiny lice began to crawl out of the ground and onto the people. Then God sent biting flies to swarm the city. Disease killed all the cattle. Ashes fell from the sky onto the people's skin and caused terrible sores to break out all over them. Hailstones and giant storms destroyed all the crops.

Before each plague, God sent Moses and Aaron to the king. But after each plague, the king still refused to free the Israelites. He would not believe God's power.

53. GOD'S FINAL PUNISHMENT

Exodus 10 - 11

The Lord sent a mighty wind from the east over the country of Egypt. It carried thousands of locusts that fed on every plant that lived. Next, he made a terrible darkness come over the land. For three days, it was so black no one could see anything.

The king called to Moses once more. "You may go but leave all your herds and flocks behind," he told him.

"When we go, we will take all that is ours with us," Moses told him.

"No," yelled the Pharaoh. "Go and do not ever see me again."

Moses knew that the Lord was going to deliver one last punishment.

God said to Moses, "At midnight I will go out into the land of Egypt and every firstborn son in all the homes will die. Even the Pharaoh's firstborn son will not be spared. There will be a great sorrow throughout Egypt."

"The Israelites will be kept safe from all of this and will not be harmed," Moses said to Pharaoh. "Then you will see how the Lord looks after his people."

The Pharaoh was as stubborn as ever so Aaron and Moses left him to go out and do what God had told them.

54. THE PASSOVER FEAST

Exodus 12

God told Moses and Aaron to meet with the leaders of Israel. They were to do what he said so they would be protected when God came through Egypt to kill the firstborn sons.

Moses told the leaders that the father of each of the Israelite families must find a lamb and kill it. The blood of the lamb must be smeared on the top and sides of the doors of their houses. Then they should roast the lamb's flesh and prepare it for a feast.

"Eat all of the meat the night of the feast," Moses told them. "When God comes in the night to find the firstborn sons, he will see the blood on your doors. He will know you are one of his people and he will pass over your house to the next."

He told them that every year they should observe the day of the Passover and remember the night the Lord saved them.

55. LEAVING EGYPT

Exodus 12

Shortly after midnight on the night of the Passover, a great cry rose up from the Egyptian people. Just as God had promised, all the firstborn sons had died. Even the firstborn cattle in the herds were dead.

The Israelites had obeyed God and stayed in their homes, eating the roast lamb. They had worn their shoes and travelling clothes to the table so they would be ready when Moses called to them.

Pharaoh sent for Moses and Aaron as soon as he discovered what had happened to the firstborn sons. He knew that this time, God had proven he was more powerful than the Pharaoh. Now he was very eager to get the Israelites out of his country.

"Get away from my people," he said. "Take your women and children and animals too. Leave my country and never come back."

So Moses sent word to the Israelites, and everyone came out of their houses and into the street. After all the disasters and plagues that the Egyptians had to endure, the Egyptians were happy to see the Israelites go. They gave the Israelites gifts to take with them.

On that very day, Moses began to lead all the people of Israel out of town, back toward the Promised Land.

56. JOURNEY TO THE RED SEA

Exodus 13 - 14

Moses and Aaron led the people of Israel according to God's chosen path. They traveled many miles in the desert before they set up camp beside the sea.

Back in Egypt, the king wanted to go back to building the great structures he had planned. But without all the Israelite slaves, there was no one to do the work. He began to regret letting the Israelite people go. So he ordered some of his army to go into the desert and bring back the Israelites.

God warned Moses that Pharaoh was sending his men after the Israelites. "Don't be afraid," God said to him. "I am with you, and I will keep my people safe."

The Israelites were sitting around their tents where they had camped by the sea. They saw a dust cloud on the horizon, and soon realized that the Egyptians were on their trail.

"Why did you bring us here?" they shouted to Moses. "Now they will kill us all."

Moses broke away from the crowd so he could pray to God.

"Why are you calling to me?" God said. "Speak to the people and tell them to follow you. But first, lift up your rod and wave it over the sea. You will escape that way."

57. A PATH THROUGH THE WATER

Exodus 14 – 15

When Moses raised the rod over the water, a very strange thing began to happen. The waves parted down the middle of the sea and soon a dry path lay at the bottom. Moses motioned for the Israelite people to follow him.

The Egyptians could see what was happening. They tried to speed up to catch the Israelites. God was against the Egyptians, though. He showed them his power by causing the wheels to fall off their chariots so they had to drag them along by hand.

After all the Israelites had crossed the sea, God told Moses to raise the rod again and wave it over the sea. Moses did as God asked and the waters of the sea began to cover the path. All the Egyptian soldiers were drowned instantly.

The Israelites rejoiced because the Lord had saved them. They began to sing a song: "I will sing to the Lord because he has triumphed gloriously; he has thrown the horse and rider into the sea."

58. GOD SENDS FOOD AND WATER

Exodus 15 - 16

Moses and the Israelites walked for many days through the desert without water. When they did find water, it tasted so bitter they could not drink it. The people cried to Moses, asking him what to do. God told Moses to throw a tree into the pool of water. Moses obeyed and the water turned sweet. Later the people began to complain to Moses because they had nothing to eat.

"We were better off in Egypt," they cried.

God spoke again to Moses. "Tell the people that they will have meat and bread when they wake up in the morning. Then they will know how good their Lord is to them."

The next morning the people looked outside their tents. They saw hundreds of birds called quail, and white, flaky dew lay over everything. The Israelites caught the quail to eat. When they touched the dew to their lips, they found it tasted just like bread.

Moses told the people that God would send enough quail and dew, which they called manna, to feed them each day.

"On the sixth day, collect enough food for two days," said Moses. "On the Sabbath, the Lord will not send any food because it is a holy day of rest."

59. MOSES AND THE ROD

Exodus 17

God had instructed Moses to take his long, wooden rod with him when he first started on the journey to free the

Israelites. So far, it had helped him perform many miracles.

Moses and the people were almost to the place where he had begun so many years ago. They stopped at a place called Rephidim which was right below Mount Horeb where God had spoken to Moses from the burning bush. Once again, the people were without water. They were hot and thirsty, and they were angry with Moses.

Moses prayed to God. "What shall I do?" he asked. "They have threatened to stone me if I do not find water for them to drink."

God told Moses to take the rod and tell the leaders to follow him up to Mount Horeb. When they arrived on the mountain, God showed Moses a rock and told him to hit it with the rod. He did, and a big stream of water began to pour out of it.

Again, God had provided for the needs of the Israelites.

60. HEAVY HANDS

Exodus 17

A group of people called Amalekites were living near the Israelite camp at Rephidim. They sent an army to attack the Israelites and take their food and water.

Moses called for one of his men named Joshua to lead an army against the enemy.

"While you are in battle," Moses said to him, "I will take the rod of the Lord and hold it over you from the hilltop. The Israelite army will be protected."

The next day, Moses, Aaron, and Hur climbed up the hill to watch the fighting. Moses stood there for many hours while the Israelite army battled the Amalekites. Soon his arms became tired, and he lowered the rod. The enemy immediately began to take the lead against the Israelites. Aaron and Hur saw what was happening. They found a large rock for Moses to sit on, and they stood on either side of him, holding up his arms.

At the end of the day, the Israelites had defeated their enemy. Moses was very grateful. He built an altar to thank God for sparing his people once again.

61. MOUNT SINAI

Exodus 18 - 19

The people of Israel were finally nearing the Promised Land. They began to settle and make camps for themselves. Eventually, arguments began to break out among the people. No matter how small the disagreement, the people hurried to Moses for help. Moses grew tired of listening to the people day after day.

One evening, Jethro, Moses' father-in-law, arrived with his wife and sons to visit Moses. He saw all the troubles Moses was having to deal with and suggested that Moses pick leaders from among the people to handle the everyday problems.

"If a really big problem comes up, then they can call on you," Jethro said.

Moses liked the idea, so he appointed some helpers. It was a good thing, too, because God would soon call Moses to do some very important work for him.

The group set up camp below Mount Sinai. This mountain reached so high in the sky that a cloud hung around the top of it. God called to Moses from that mountain with a message to tell the people of Israel.

"Tell my people that I have brought them out of Egypt because I love them," God said. "I have taken care of them, but now it is time for them to obey me. I will tell them some special rules they will have to follow. If they will obey, they will be my most treasured people on earth."

62. COMMANDMENTS FROM GOD

Exodus 19 - 20

Moses told the people they should be ready for God's call. They followed Moses to the foot of Mount Sinai. He told them to stay there and listen for the sound of a trumpet. Then Moses went up the mountain. There God gave him the Ten Commandments for the people to follow. Because God made the earth and the people on it, God knew what would really make them happy. The first commandments were to help people know how to be closer to God.

1. I am your God, and you must not worship other gods.
2. Don't make up any idols or images to worship or serve.
3. Never take God's name in vain.
4. Remember the sabbath day and keep it holy.

63. RULES FOR LIVING WITH OTHERS

Exodus 20

God knew about the trouble people had getting along with one another. The other commandments he gave Moses on

51

Mount Sinai were to help people treat one another kindly.

5. We must obey and respect our father and our mother.
6. We must not kill one another.
7. We must not commit adultery.
8. We must not steal from one another.
9. We must not tell lies about each other.
10. We must not want something that belongs to someone else.

God gave Moses two stone tablets that had his commandments carved in them. Moses kept these as reminders of God's laws for his people.

64. THE COVENANT

Exodus 21 - 24

The Ten Commandments were God's most important instructions to the people. There were many rules to help guide the Israelites in their daily lives.

God called Moses to Mount Sinai again to hear the covenant made many hundreds of years ago with Abraham. God had done all the things he told Moses he would do. Now he wanted to make a convenant with the people of Israel.

Moses stayed on the mountain for forty days and nights, copying down what God told him. He read to the people all the commandments God wished them to keep.

"If you will keep these laws," Moses told them, "God has promised that you will be a special people."

The people said that they would obey God, so Moses built a big altar and sacrificed some of the animals. Then he took the blood and sprinkled it on the people to remind them of their convenant with God.

65. A TENT FOR WORSHIP

Exodus 25 - 31

During the long years that Moses and his people had been on the road, they had stopped occasionally to build an altar to give special thanks to God. But they had no building or set place in which to worship. God told Moses that it was time for the Israelites to build a tent to serve as a place of worship. They would call it a tabernacle. It would be easy to take apart and put back together so they could take it with them on their journey.

God described exactly how the tent was to be built and what would go inside it. Many materials were needed to create the tent. When the people found out what Moses wanted them to build, they gladly donated the wood and cloth and precious metals that the Egyptians had given them. The inside would have beautiful curtains. Behind one set of curtains would be a special chest of gold and wood called the mercy seat.

Aaron was to be the leader of the worship services. He and his sons would have special clothes to show they were priests. They would make offerings on the altar to show the people's love and obedience for the Lord.

66. THE GOLDEN CALF

Exodus 32

Moses had patiently written down everything God had told him. Now it was time for him to take the two stone tablets and return to camp.

He believed the people would be eager to hear about all the wonderful things God had told him. Moses had been gone a long time, though. The people had become very restless. One day they had complained to Aaron about having to stay in one place for so long.

"We have not seen Moses for weeks," they said. "Make us a god who can finish leading us on this journey."

Aaron told them to bring their wives' and daughters' golden earrings to him. He melted them down and molded a golden calf. Then he built an altar in front of it. The next morning the people brought offerings to their new god. They brought out food and drink, and Aaron proclaimed it a feast to the Lord.

God could see and hear everything that was happening. He became very angry and told Moses he would destroy the people for breaking his commandment. Moses begged him to forgive the people of Israel. Then he went down the mountain to find out what was going on.

When Moses saw the people drunk and dancing before the golden statue, he threw down the two tablets God had given him, and they broke into pieces. He ordered them to grind up the idol, and he made them swallow the dust.

67. A NEW CONVENANT

Exodus 33 - 34

Moses went back to beg God to forgive the Israelites for worshiping the golden calf.

"Those who have sinned will be punished," God said.

Moses offered to take all the sins of the people on himself. God saw that Moses was very sincere about helping his people.

Moses went back to camp and set up the tabernacle. The people watched him go inside. They saw the cloud from the top of Mount Sinai come down and lie in front of the tabernacle tent. The people were much afraid because they knew that God was present in the cloud.

Moses said to God: "How can we go on with this journey if you will not go with us? No one will believe we are your special people."

"I will go with you as you ask," God said to him. "You have been a faithful servant."

So Moses carved out two new tablets of stone and took them back to Mount Sinai. There God replaced the two tablets he had broken.

Moses stayed with God on the mountain for forty days and nights. When he came down again, Moses' face was shining with light. He and all the people of Israel were very thankful that God had given them another chance.

68. THE LORD'S TABERNACLE

Exodus 35 - 40

The Israelites were ready to do whatever God asked of them. Moses told them to prepare to work six days a week on the tabernacle. No one would work on the seventh day, which was the holy sabbath.

Moses asked for offerings to go into the tabernacle. People brought gold and silver jewelry and precious stones. Skilled carpenters began to carve the tables and altars. They hung beautiful blue, purple, and red draperies as God had said. This time Moses knew the tabernacle would at last be completed.

The great cloud the people had seen many times on their journey came again to their camp. It hung over the tabernacle and glowed so brightly the people could not go inside.

The next morning the cloud lifted from the tabernacle and began to move. This was a sign to the people that the Lord was with them, and they were to continue on their journey together. When the cloud stopped again, the people stopped, too. They put up the tabernacle and went inside to worship.

69. RULES FOR FOOD AND FEASTS

Leviticus 11 - 25

Many of the rules God gave his people were to help them in their daily lives. God wanted his people to be clean and healthy. He told them what foods they should eat and which animals and birds to kill for food.

God asked his people to remember him with some special feasts every year. They would remember the Passover by eating bread without yeast for seven days and with a worship service on the first and last day. In this way the people were to show their thanks to God for saving them from the Egyptians and bringing them to the Promised Land.

The Israelites were to give thanks at a Harvest Feast for all the crops they raised each year. Then on the seventh year they would plant no crops and let the land rest. They called this the sabbath year. God told them that after seven sabbath years had passed, the fiftieth year would be a Year of Jubilee. It would be a whole year of forgiveness and joy.

70. THE PEOPLE COMPLAIN

Numbers 11 - 12

Over 600,000 people had begun the journey from Egypt with Moses. Some of them seemed to be unhappy or dissatisfied all the time. The unhappy people did a lot of complaining.

It made God very angry when the people complained. He had done many wonderful things for them, but they quickly forgot them. Not long after they left Mount Sinai, the people began to complain because they were tired of eating the manna that God provided every day.

"I will send the people meat for a whole month," God told Moses. "They will have so much of it, it will make them sick."

The next day a flock of quail flew into the camp. There were so many, the people stayed up for two days gathering them to eat. The people who had complained the most ate too much of the meat. They got sick and died. It was a hard lesson for everyone.

71. SPIES IN THE PROMISED LAND

Numbers 13 - 14

Moses led his people to the borders of Canaan, the Promised Land. As God had instructed him, he sent a group of men from the camp as spies to go into Canaan and see what the land and the people were like.

After nearly six weeks, the spies returned. They brought with them all kinds of beautiful fruits.

"It is a lovely land, indeed," they said. "The people seem very happy there. They are big and strong. If we try to take the land, they will kill us."

Caleb and Joshua were two of the spies who had gone with the others. "Yes, the people are mighty," they said, "but we have nothing to fear. God promised us this country. He will take care of us."

But the people saw the other spies shaking their heads in disagreement. "We have come all this way from Egypt just so the Canaanites can kill us," they said to Moses. They complained louder and louder.

God didn't like their complaints and threatened again to destroy the Israelites. But after Moses begged for mercy, God spared all but the ten spies who had given a bad report.

72. TROUBLE IN THE DESERT

Numbers 16 - 17

Shortly after they returned to the desert, a man named Korah got some of his friends and some of the Israelite leaders to rebel against Moses. When Moses heard what they were up to, he told them to come to the tabernacle the next day with a cup for burning incense.

A great crowd gathered around Korah and his men. Moses and Aaron stood to one side and Korah on the other.

"God will now show you who should be your leaders," Moses said to the people. "If these men live, then I am not the one. But if the earth opens to take them, you will know that God has chosen Aaron and me."

Just then the ground underneath Korah opened up and swallowed him and all his men.

The Israelites began to think that what had happened to Korah was Moses' fault. A group of them headed for the tabernacle. As they came nearer, the cloud of the Lord appeared over the tent. Moses and Aaron fell on their faces before the cloud. Moses prayed that God would forgive his people.

Then God told Moses to get a rod from each one of the twelve tribal leaders and lay them before the tabernacle. Moses obeyed, and the next day Aaron's rod had sprouted leaves and fruit. That was God's message to the people that Aaron was his chosen leader of the tabernacle.

73. MOSES DISOBEYS

Numbers 20

After many days in the desert, the people again ran out of water. As they always did, they went to Moses for help.

"You have brought us out of Egypt to this evil place," they cried. "Now we will die because there is no water."

God told Moses to take his rod and go to a nearby rock.

"Speak to the rock so they can all hear you," he said. "Water will come out of the rock so everyone can get a drink."

Moses went up to the rock, but instead of speaking to it, he took his rod and hit it twice.

"Listen, you rebels," he shouted. "Must I always get your water for you!"

Water poured from the rock as God said it would. God spoke to Moses and Aaron: "I asked you to speak to the rock, but you hit it. If you cannot obey me in front of my people, you will not lead them to the Promised Land."

Then God told Moses to take Aaron and his son Eleazar to the top of Mount Hov. There Aaron died, and his son took his place as priest. All the people were sad at Aaron's death and mourned him for 30 days.

74. THE SNAKES

Numbers 21

Many years passed and still the people of Israel wandered through the desert. Before long, the people began to complain again. "We have no bread and very little water," they said to Moses. "Surely we will die in this desert."

God heard the people complaining again to Moses. He sent many poisonous snakes into the camp. The snakes seemed to come from everywhere. They bit many of the Israelites and some of them died. Moses prayed to God that he would take the snakes away.

"Make a serpent of brass," God said to Moses. "Then put it on a stake that is high enough for everyone to see. Anyone who has been bitten will look at the brass snake and live."

Those people who believed what Moses told them about the brass snake came to look up at it. They were healed of their snake bites because they had faith in God.

75. BALAAM'S DONKEY

Numbers 22 - 24

The people traveled to a place called Moab where they pitched their tents. Balak was the king of the Moabite people. He was frightened when he learned that the Israelites were so close because they outnumbered his army.

Balak sent messengers to a wise man called Balaam. They offered him a lot of gold if he would go and place curses on the Israelites. At first Balaam refused. The Lord had told him that the Israelites were blessed people. King Balak sent more gold for Balaam and finally he gave in.

Balaam climbed on his donkey for the trip to the Israelites' camp. The donkey stopped several times on the road and would go no farther. Balaam got off and beat the donkey. He did not see the angel of God that the donkey had seen.

"What have I done to make you beat me?" the donkey said.

Balaam was shocked as he listened to the donkey. Then he saw the angel of God. He was very ashamed because he knew he was doing something God had told him not to do.

"Go on to the Israelites' camp," the angel said to him. "But speak only what the Lord tells you to speak."

76. PLANS FOR A NEW LAND

Numbers 25 - 26

The journey to the Promised Land was almost over. God told the people to prepare to cross the Jordan River. Moses and one of the priests counted all the men in the twelve tribes who were twenty or older.

Then he led them into battle against the people of Midian, because they had talked the Israelites into worshiping idols many years before. The Israelite soldiers destroyed all the Midianites. They took their animals and offered their jewels as a gift to God for protecting them in battle.

Moses described to the people how they were to divide the land of Canaan among the tribes. They were also to establish six special cities called cities of refuge and cities of safety. A person who killed another accidently could go to a city of safety. There they would be protected from anyone seeking revenge for the killing. Murderers would not be allowed inside a city of safety because they would have broken one of God's Ten Commandments.

77. MOSES' LAST SPEECH

Deuteronomy

It was time for the people to cross over the Jordan River into the Promised Land. Because Moses had disobeyed God by hitting at the rock with his stick, he would not be making the last part of the journey with his people.

Moses gathered the people of Israel together one last time. He repeated the Ten Commandments to them. Moses also reminded the people of all God had done for them over this long journey.

Then God spoke to Moses. "Although you will never go into the land, you will see it before you die," God said. "Climb to the top of Mount Pisgah, and there you will see the Promised Land before you die."

Moses did as God had told him. He told the people to welcome Joshua as their new leader. Then he went up on the mountain where he died. The people of Israel cried and mourned for Moses for thirty days after he died. He was the greatest leader in Israel's history.

78. JOSHUA LEADS THE ISRAELITES

Joshua 1

God came to speak to Joshua: "My servant Moses is dead. Now you must lead my people across the river."

Joshua listened to God's instructions. He had stood beside Moses throughout the journey to the Promised Land. He knew all the problems and hard times that Moses had to face.

"Don't worry, I will be with you as I was with Moses," God said to Joshua. "You must be brave and keep my laws. I will make you the leader of this new land."

Joshua spoke to the leaders of the tribes, telling them to be ready to go into the land that God had given them. All the people agreed that they would follow Joshua's orders.

"We will follow you as we followed Moses," they said. "Whoever rebels against your orders will be put to death."

79. RAHAB AND THE SPIES

Joshua 2

Before he sent the armies of Israel across the Jordan River, Joshua sent two more men over to spy on the Canaanites. News of the spies soon reached the king of Jericho. He knew they would be stopping at an inn owned by a woman named

Rahab. The king told her to watch for the two. But when the spies arrived, Rahab hid them from the king's soldiers.

"The men were here," she told the soldiers, "but they left. If you go quickly, you may catch them."

The two spies crawled out of the straw on the roof where Rahab had hidden them. They wondered why Rahab had gone against her king to protect them.

"I have heard what your powerful God has done for you," she said. "Since I have saved you, will you also save me and my family when your armies come to take the land?"

The men agreed. Then Rahab lowered a long rope out a window at the back of the inn. The spies climbed down to the street and gave Rahab instructions. When the Israelite armies come to Canaan, hang a red cord in your window," they said. "Stay in your house and do not come out. No harm will come to you."

80. ACROSS THE JORDAN

Joshua 3 - 4

When the spies returned, they told the people what had happened to them.

"Surely God means for us to have this land," they said. "The people are frightened of us."

Joshua called all the people to come to the river. The water was very high, and it looked dangerous to cross. Joshua told the priests carrying the ark to go first.

They stepped into the rushing water and it stopped flowing. By the time they were halfway across, it had dried up completely! The priests stood there with the ark while the people crossed the dry riverbed safely to the other side.

Joshua asked the twelve leaders of the tribes who had crossed the river first to bring him twelve stones. They used the stones to build a monument beside the river.

"When your children ask you what this monument is for," said Joshua, "Tell them it is to remember the time that God dried up the riverbed so the people of Israel could cross into their Promised Land. Then all the people of the earth will know how powerful your God is."

81. ORDERS FROM GOD

Joshua 5 - 6

Joshua thought about what he must do to win the battle against the Canaanites. One day he looked up and saw a man with a sword standing in front of him.

"Are you one of our men or one of the enemies?" he asked.

"I am a soldier of the Lord," the man replied.

Joshua fell down to worship the stranger. God had sent him with instructions for taking of the city of Jericho.

God told Joshua to pick seven priests to march in the middle of the army. They were to circle the city for seven days, blowing trumpets as they went.

Joshua sent the priests and soldiers to the city walls to do what God had asked. On the seventh day, the priests blew their trumpets as they made their way around the city for the seventh time and the people gave a great shout. Suddenly, the walls of Jericho fell to the ground. The Israelite soldiers rushed in. They saw the red cord in the window of Rahab's inn. They took her and her family away and burned the city.

82. A THIEF IN THE CAMP

Joshua 7

The victory over Jericho was exciting. When it came time to take the next city, the people were ready to go into battle. Joshua sent spies into the city of Ai. They reported that the army there was small. Only a few thousand Israelite soldiers would be needed to defeat them.

Joshua sent his men into the city, but the soldiers of Ai attacked and killed many of them. Joshua fell on his knees to God when he heard the news.

"Why did this happen to us?" he cried. "Why did you bring us here to be killed. No one will believe we are your chosen people."

God told Joshua that one of his men had taken some jewels out of Jericho after God had told them not to. That was why they had lost the battle at Ai.

Joshua found the one who had sinned, a man named Achan. He confessed, and Joshua sent a messenger to his tent for the stolen items. Achan and his family were punished.

Then God said to Joshua: "Take your soldiers to Ai. This time the city will be yours."

83. A TREATY WITH THE GIBEONITES

Joshua 9

The leaders of Canaan began to hear about the Israelite victories. They knew that unless they did something to stop them, the Israelites would take over the whole country.

The people of Gibeon decided they must find a way to make peace with the Israelites. Some of them disguised themselves as strangers from a faraway land. They wore old clothes and carried stale bread to look as if they had been traveling a long time.

The Gibeonites rode into the Israelite camp and asked to see Joshua. "We have heard of your great victories," they said. "We would like to make a peace treaty with you."

"We cannot make a treaty with you," Joshua told them. "God has told us to destroy all the people of Canaan because they don't believe in him."

Then the Gibeonites took the stale bread out of their packs.

"We are not from this country. Look at this old bread. We have traveled from far away," they said.

Joshua did not ask for God's advice before he spoke to the Gibeonites. Instead, he agreed to sign a peace treaty with them. A few days later, Joshua found out that the Gibeonites had lied to him. The people of Israel wanted to kill the Gibeonites, but Joshua told them they must honor the treaty.

84. THE SUN STANDS STILL

Joshua 10

Word spread about the Gibeonites' trick on the people of Israel. The king of Jerusalem feared the people of Gibeon would join forces with the Israelites and attack his city. He asked the leaders of four other cities to send their armies to attack Gibeon.

The Gibeonites pleaded with Joshua to help them defeat the armies. Joshua didn't want to help them because they had lied to him. Then God told Joshua that if he would keep his promise to the people of Gibeon, God would go with him into battle.

The Israelite army attacked the enemies, and the fighting went on all day. Late in the afternoon, Joshua was afraid he would lose the battle in the darkness. He prayed for the sun to stand still over Gibeon, and God answered his prayer. For a whole day the sun didn't move over Gibeon, and the moon stayed over the valley of Aijalon.

Joshua and his army were able to claim all the land for Israel because God had helped them in the battle.

85. DIVIDING UP THE LAND

Joshua 13 - 22

Finally, the people of Israel had destroyed the evil Canaanites and driven them out of the Promised Land of Israel. It was time for the land to be divided among the twelve tribes. The tribe of Levi did not receive a portion because they were to stay with the tabernacle. They were instructed to take the tabernacle to the city of Shiloh where it was to stay from then on. Then God gave the Levites special cities where they could live with their families.

The people in the tribe of Reuben asked to go back to their families across the Jordan River. They were very grateful to be going back to the good pasture land they had chosen earlier. They stopped by the river and built an altar.

"We want to remind everyone that we are Israelites, too, even though we have settled on the other side of the river."

All the people were satisfied in their new homes. God had made good his promise to Jacob many years ago that he would lead the children of Abraham into the Promised Land.

86. TIME TO CHOOSE

Joshua 24

After everyone had settled in their new lands, Joshua called the leaders together. Many days had passed since Joshua had taken command of the journey to the Promised Land. He had grown very old and would soon die.

"Now is the time for you to choose whom you will serve," he said to the people.

Joshua reminded the Israelites of all the good things that God had done for them from the time of Abraham to their recent victories over the Canaanites.

"If you want to follow the Lord," Joshua said, "you must worship only him. Put away all your false gods and idols."

The people promised to serve only God, so Joshua made a covenant with them to keep their promise. He took a large stone and placed it under an oak tree.

"This stone will be a witness to all we have said today," he told them.

Not long after Joshua had made his covenant with the people, he passed away. They buried him on the hillside in his own part of the new land.

87. LEADERS FOR ISRAEL

Judges 1 - 2

Before Joshua died, the Israelites had obeyed the laws of God. They had destroyed the Canaanite tribes as God had told them. Then a new generation came to power in the Promised Land. Many of these people did not grow up in the time of Joshua, so they didn't know about God and the commandments.

Eventually, the people began to make friends with the Canaanites. The more the people of Israel stayed near the Canaanites, the more they began to act like them. This was very bad because the Canaanite tribes worshiped idols. They sacrificed their children so their crops would grow well.

God was angry with the people. They could no longer withstand their enemies who attacked them and took their possessions. The people of Israel asked God for forgiveness and help.

God knew his people needed someone to guide them in their everyday lives. He sent fifteen different leaders to guide the Israelites. These people were called judges, and they helped the people rely on God's power.

88. JUDGES FOR THE PEOPLE

Judges 3

The first of the judges that God sent to lead his people was named Othniel. He rescued the Israelites from the king of Mesopotamia who was keeping them as slaves. The people obeyed Othniel and followed God's rules for forty years.

After Othniel died, the Israelites went back to doing as they pleased. Soon they came under the power of the Moabite king, Eglon. He was mean and selfish and made the Israelites pay most of their taxes in crops.

The Israelites prayed for another leader to save them from King Eglon. God appointed Ehud, a man from the tribe of Benjamin, as the next judge for the Israelites.

Ehud went with the servants to pay taxes to King Eglon. He hid a knife in his clothes and once inside the palace, he stabbed the king. Then he escaped and ran to tell the Israelite soldiers to attack the Moabites.

Another forty years of peace came to the Israelites under Ehud's leadership.

Next God sent a new judge named Shamgar. Each time the people of Israel forgot God's laws, they lost their freedom. But God always heard their pleas for help.

89. WOMEN OF VICTORY

Judges 4 - 5

The Israelites came under the rule of King Jabin. He had a large army with 900 chariots. The leader of this army was a man called Sisera. He treated the Israelites badly because he knew the Israelite army was small.

Deborah was a prophet and judge for the Israelites. She helped them solve many of their problems. One day God came to her with a message. Then she called a man named Barak.

"God asked me to call for you," she told him. "You are to lead an army against Sisera and his men."

Barak told Deborah that he would go only if she would go with him. Together they gathered an army to attack Sisera. When the battle started, heavy rain began to fall on the battlefield. The chariots carrying Sisera's men started sinking into the mud. The Israelite soldiers surrounded the chariots and defeated Sisera's army.

Sisera escaped the fighting. He ran until he could run no more. He saw a tent and asked the woman inside for a drink of water. The woman, named Jael, knew Sisera was her people's enemy. She invited him inside to rest, and when he fell asleep, she killed him. Barak came looking for Sisera later, and he was surprised that a brave woman had helped him once again.

90. GOD'S CALL TO GIDEON

Judges 6

For many years the Midianite tribes attacked the Israelites just as their crops were ready to harvest. They would come down from the mountains and take everything they could get their hands on. When the Israelites saw them coming, they ran to caves in the hills. After they came back out, they saw that all their food was gone.

The Israelites were hungry and scared. When they could stand it no longer, they cried out to God to help them.

God called a young man named Gideon to lead his people. "The Lord is with you," a voice said to him. Gideon looked up to see an angel of the Lord standing before him. "If the Lord is with us," Gideon said to the angel, "then why have all these bad things happened to us?"

"I have come to send you to save the Israelites from the Midianites," answered the angel.

"I cannot save Israel," Gideon said. "I am only a poor farm boy."

The Lord spoke through the angel and told Gideon that he would be by his side in the battle against the Midianites.

91. A SIGN TO GIDEON

Judges 6

Gideon brought the angel an offering of meat, bread, and broth. He did as the angel said and put the meat and bread on a rock. Then he poured the broth over it.

The angel of the Lord touched the offering with his wooden staff, and it caught on fire and burned up. Gideon knew then that he was in the presence of the Lord.

"Now go down to the village," God said to him. "Find the altar to the god Baal and break it down. Then build an altar to the Lord and sacrifice one of your father's young bulls."

Gideon did as God said. The next morning, the men of the city could see what had been done to their altar. They came looking for Gideon.

"Gideon must die for what he has done," they said.

Gideon's father heard the men yelling outside his door.

"Why must you speak up for Baal?" he said to them. "If Baal is a true god, he should be able to speak for himself."

The men had no reply for that. They let Gideon go free, and he was very grateful.

92. GIDEON'S ARMY

Judges 7

Gideon gathered many thousands of Israelite soldiers to-gether to take on the Midianites, but God thought Gideon had too many soldiers. "If you win the battle," God said, "people will say it was because of the mighty army. I want them to know that I am the one who will save them."

Then God told Gideon to let all the soldiers who were scared of fighting go back home. Gideon gave the order, and nearly two-thirds of the men left.

"There are still too many," God said. "Tell the men to go to the stream and take a drink of water." Some of Gideon's men put their faces in the water and sucked it into their mouths. Others reached in with their hands and cupped the water up to their lips.

"The second group is the one you will take into battle," God told Gideon.

There were only 300 men left to fight the Midianites. The next morning, Gideon handed each of his men a trumpet and clay pitcher with a lamp in it, and gave them instructions. The soldiers reached the enemy camp that night. Gideon gave the signal, and they blew on their trumpets and threw down the lamps. Then they all shouted, "The sword of the Lord and of Gideon!"

The Midianite soldiers panicked when they heard all the noise. They began to fight among themselves. Then they took off into the hills. The Israelites had defeated their enemies without even fighting.

93. JEPHTHAH MAKES A PROMISE

Judges 11

A tribe called the Ammonites attacked the Israelites because the Israelites had taken some of their land when they settled in the Promised Land. The Israelites needed someone to lead an army to fight the Ammonites. The bravest fighter in the land was a man called Jephthah.

When word reached Jephthah that his relatives wanted him to lead the army, Jephthah asked them about the reward for his efforts. "If I lead this army to victory over the Ammonites, will you make me the leader of your city when I return?"

The people agreed to do as Jephthah asked. Now Jephthah had to be sure he won the battle so he would be king.

Jephthah decided to bargain with the Lord. He promised God that he would sacrifice the first thing he saw when he came home from battle if God would let his army win.

As he had asked, Jephthah's army defeated the Ammonites. When he came back home, his only child was standing at the door to greet him. Jephthah ran to hug his daughter; then he remembered the bargain he had made with God.

In trying to bribe God, Jephthah had ended up losing the thing that was most precious to him.

94. SAMSON IS BORN

Judges 13

The Philistines came again to attack the Israelites and take over their land. They made life hard for the people of Israel. The people hoped and prayed for another great leader to come and free them.

A man named Manoah lived with his wife among the Israelite tribes. The couple had no children, and they wanted a baby more than anything else.

God sent a messenger to Manoah's wife: "Soon you will have a baby," the messenger said. "He will grow up to free Israel from the rule of the Philistines."

The angel told Manoah's wife that the child was to be a Nazarite. That was a group who served God in a special way. They left their hair long and did not cut it until their service to God was completed.

Manoah's wife told her husband all that the angel had said. Manoah offered a sacrifice to God on an altar. The sacrifice burst into flames as soon as it touched the altar. Manoah was frightened by the fire and ran back into the house.

"Don't be afraid," said his wife. "The fire is a sign that the Lord accepted your sacrifice. He has come to tell us the wonderful things that will take place."

Some months later, Manoah's wife gave birth to a son, and they named him Samson.

95. SAMSON AND THE LION

Judges 14

As Samson grew older, his parents discovered that he was much stronger than the other children his age. He was strong-willed, too. One day he came home to announce his plans to marry a Philistine girl.

Samson's father, Manoah, was very upset by this news. He

wanted his son to marry an Israelite girl. Samson wouldn't listen to his parents. "This girl pleases me," he said.

The three of them set off to visit the girl's parents. On the way, Samson heard a noise in some bushes near the road. He went over to see about the noise and found a young lion crouched and waiting to jump on him!

Samson grabbed the lion with both hands and killed him. He walked back to the road and joined his parents, but he didn't say anything about what had happened.

When he went back to the girl's home again, he stopped by the place where he had killed the lion. Only the bones were there with a swarm of bees flying all around them. Samson reached in the carcass and took some honey in his hands. He ate some and took some to his parents, but Samson never told them where it came from.

96. THE RIDDLE

Judges 14

Samson was arranging for his wedding feast. He called all the young men aside.

"I will give you new clothes if you can answer this riddle: Out of the eater came meat, and out of the strong came sweetness," Samson said.

The young men went to Samson's bride and told her that unless she found out the answer to the riddle for them, they would destroy her house. The girl was frightened by their threats. She begged Samson to tell her the answer.

The feast went on for a week. By the last day, Samson could not stand to listen to his bride's sobbing any longer. He told her the answer to the riddle, and she ran and told the men.

"We know the answer to your riddle," the men said to Samson. "What is sweeter than honey, and what is stronger than a lion?"

Samson knew there was only one way the men could know the answer—his wife. After he had given the men the clothes he had promised them, he went home to Israel without her. He did not want a wife he couldn't trust.

97. A STRING OF FOXES

Judges 15

One day Samson decided to go back and see his wife. When he started to go into her tent, her father told him he could not be with her because he had given her to one of Samson's men.

In his anger, Samson went out and caught 300 foxes. He tied them together by their tails. Then he tied a burning torch between the tails of each pair of foxes. He let the foxes loose in the fields and vineyards belonging to the Philistines.

When the people discovered that their crops were on fire, they demanded to know who had done such a thing. Someone told them about Samson and what had happened to his bride. The Philistines blamed the bride and her father for starting the trouble and killed them.

Samson attacked the Philistines again after he found out they had killed his wife. Then he took a vow that he would not seek more vengeance.

98. A SECRET STRENGTH

Judges 16

For twenty years, Samson served as a judge and leader for the Israelites. It was many years since he had taken his Philistine wife. He met a beautiful woman named Delilah one day and fell in love with her.

Soon the Philistines came to ask Delilah for her help.

"If you can find out what makes Samson so strong," they said to her, "we will each give you 1,100 pieces of silver."

Delilah wanted to be a very rich woman, so she asked Samson to tell her the secret of his strength.

Samson told Delilah that if he was tied up with seven leather strings, he would become weak. That night Delilah tied Samson as he had said. She told the Philistines to wait in the next room. Then she shouted to Samson that the Philistines were coming after him. He leaped up from his sleep and the strings snapped like twigs.

Delilah asked Samson again what his secret was. He told her that only new rope must be used to tie him. Then he said that if his hair was braided a certain way he would lose his strength. However, Samson stayed as strong as ever, and the Philistines could not capture him.

99. SAMSON'S WEAKNESS

Judges 16

Delilah was growing very impatient.

"How can you say that you love me?" she said to him

one day. "You have teased me so many times. Surely, your heart is not with me."

She cried and begged until Samson gave in.

"A razor has never touched my hair," he explained to her. "I have been a Nazarite in service to God since my birth. If my hair is cut off, I will no longer have my great strength."

Delilah wasted no time getting word to the Philistines.

"Come quickly," she said. "This time he has told me the truth."

They brought the money they had promised her, and went to hide in the next room. When Samson had fallen asleep, Delilah called for one of the men to bring a razor and cut Samson's hair.

"The Philistines have come for you," Delilah shouted.

Samson got to his feet, but his strength was gone. The Philistines tied him and took him back to the town of Gaza.

100. SAMSON'S LAST REVENGE

Judges 16

Samson's captors put him in prison. They blinded him and bound him with heavy brass chains. He stayed in the prison for a long time, and while he was there, his hair grew long again.

The Philistines were happy to have finally caught Samson. They planned a great feast and offered a sacrifice to their god, Dagon. After they became very drunk, they shouted for Samson to be brought out so they could see their prize catch.

A young boy was sent to guide Samson out of the prison. Samson asked the boy to tie him between the two great pillars so he could lean on them and rest. The boy obeyed. Samson listened to the people laughing and shouting mean things at him. He prayed to God to help him one last time.

"Oh, Lord, remember me and give me my strength, so I may punish these Philistines who took away my sight."

Samson began to push against the two pillars as hard as he could. The pillars cracked in two, and the great building where the Philistines had gathered for their feast crumbled on top of them.

The Lord had answered Samson's last prayer.

101. RUTH FOLLOWS NAOMI

Ruth 1

One time a great famine took place in Israel. Many people had to move to another country to find food. A man called Elimelech decided to move his family to Moab. Not long after they arrived, Elimelech died. His wife, Naomi, and their two sons stayed on in Moab.

The boys grew up and married two Moabite girls, Orpah and Ruth. They all lived together until both of the sons passed away, too. Naomi was very sad. She did not like living in a strange land. Once she heard that the famine was over in Israel, Naomi started back to her homeland.

Naomi said to her daughters-in-law, "You must go back to your mothers' homes now. Someday you will meet other men and marry again."

The two girls did not want to leave Naomi, but she insisted. Finally, Orpah said good-bye to her mother-in-law and turned around to go home.

"Orpah is going, you must go, too," Naomi told Ruth.

"I want to go wherever you go," Ruth said. "I will live with you in Bethlehem and worship your God."

102. GRAIN FOR RUTH

Ruth 2

Ruth and Naomi were very poor when they returned to Bethlehem. In order to get food, Ruth went out in the fields where the farmers grew extra grain to be given to the poor. She walked behind some reapers to get their leftovers.

Boaz, the man who owned the field, stopped by to see how things were going. He asked one of his workers about the young woman who was following behind his reapers.

"That is the Moabite girl who came back here with Naomi," the servant told him.

Boaz called Ruth over to him. "Stay in my fields," he said. "I have told the reapers not to harm you. You may eat and drink whenever you wish."

Ruth hurried home at the end of the day to tell Naomi about her good fortune. Naomi asked which fields Ruth had gone to. When she told her, Naomi replied, "That man is our nearest kin. The Lord has blessed us."

103. RUTH MARRIES BOAZ

Ruth 3 - 4

Harvest time was nearly over. Every day, Ruth had gone out to Boaz's field, but now their source of food would soon be gone.

"Tonight is the night of the harvest feast," Naomi said to Ruth. "You must go to the threshing floor and lie down at Boaz's feet until he has finished eating and drinking."

Ruth waited until the feast was over, then she went to where Boaz slept. Boaz woke up and looked down at her. "Who are you?" he asked.

Ruth told him that he was her kin. She asked if he would cover her with his coat. Boaz knew what she was really asking. Since she was a widow, her next closest male relative was supposed to take her in.

"You are a good woman, Ruth, and I want to marry you," Boaz said to her. He married her and took her to live with him, and soon a baby boy was born to them.

"This child will give you much joy," the village women told Naomi. "Some day his name will be famous in Israel."

They called the child Obed, and his grandson became the great King David.

104. HANNAH'S PRAYER

1 Samuel 1

Each year an Israelite named Elkanah would bring his two wives and his children to Shiloh to worship. His wives were named Hannah and Peninnah. All his children belonged to Peninnah. Hannah had never been able to have children.

Elkanah offered many gifts to Peninnah, but he saved the best gifts for Hannah because he loved her the most. Peninnah knew how her husband felt. She said mean things to Hannah about the fact that Hannah didn't have children.

On one visit to Shiloh, the family had sat down to have their evening meal. Peninnah had treated Hannah so badly all day that she had lost her appetite. Finally, Hannah got up from the table and went back to the temple to pray.

"O Lord, if you will give me a son, then I will make him a special servant to you all of his life." Hannah made a vow to the Lord because she knew she needed God's help.

105. SAMUEL IS BORN

1 Samuel 1

The high priest named Eli was watching Hannah pray. He saw her lips move, but he heard no sound come out. He thought she must have drunk too much wine.

"I've had nothing to drink," Hannah said to Eli. "I have come here to pour out my heart to the Lord."

"Go in peace then," said the priest. "May the Lord give you what you have asked of him."

The Lord did give Hannah what she had asked for. When her son was born, she named him Samuel because that meant she had asked the Lord for him.

Hannah kept Samuel home with her for several years while the rest of the family went on their yearly journeys to the temple in Shiloh. She knew that this was the only time she would get to spend with her son because she had promised him to God as his servant.

106. RETURN TO THE TEMPLE

1 Samuel 1 – 2

When Samuel was old enough, Hannah took him back to see the old priest named Eli, who had been at the temple the night she prayed to God.

"This is the child I prayed for that night you saw me here," Hannah said to him. "I have come to do as I promised and give him over to God's service."

Eli welcomed the little boy. His own two sons did not believe in God, so he needed someone to help him offer the sacrifice. Little Samuel performed his tasks in the temple as if he had been born to do them, which in a way he had.

Hannah came back each year to see her son. She always brought him a beautiful new coat to wear. Eli knew that she missed her son, so he asked God to bless her and her husband with more children. Over the years, God answered their prayers and Hannah had three more sons and two daughters.

107. SAMUEL'S CALLING

1 Samuel 3

Eli came to rely on Samuel more as he grew older. The old priest's sight had become very weak. At night he went to his room and left Samuel out in the temple to guard the ark of the Lord.

Samuel lay asleep one night when suddenly he woke to hear someone calling his name.

"Here I am," said Samuel. He ran into Eli's room, thinking that the old man had called him.

"I didn't call you," said Eli. "Go back and lie down."

Samuel went back to his bed. He had barely gone back to sleep when he heard the voice again.

"Here I am," he said as he walked into Eli's bedroom.

"I haven't called you," said Eli. "Now go back to bed."

Again, Samuel heard someone calling his name. This time Eli knew who was calling Samuel.

"When you hear the voice," Eli told him, "say 'Speak, Lord. Your servant hears you.' Then you will hear what God wants you to know."

108. MOVING THE ARK

1 Samuel 4

Once again the Philistines gathered an army together and declared war on the Israelites. The first battle was fought and the Philistines won.

"Why has the Lord allowed our enemies to win a battle against us?" the Israelites asked. "Let us bring the ark of the covenant from Shiloh. When the Philistines see that we have it with us in our camp, they will know God is on our side."

The people of Israel shouted and cheered when they saw the ark being carried into the army camp. No one remembered that they were breaking a law by taking the ark out of Shiloh. They had forgotten God's rules.

109. THE ARK IS CAPTURED

1 Samuel 4

The Philistines were frightened when they heard that the Israelites planned to take the ark of the convenant into battle with them. They decided to fight harder than ever.

The Philistines' efforts paid off. They defeated the Israelites and captured the ark. Thirty thousand Israelite soldiers were killed in the battle including two sons of the priest Eli.

A messenger ran to Shiloh to tell about the terrible defeat. Eli was waiting by the road with the others to hear the news.

"The Israelites have fled from the Philistines," the messenger said. "Many of our soldiers were killed, including your two sons. And worst of all, the Philistines took the ark with them."

The news of the ark and his sons was too much for the old man to take. He fell over backwards off his seat, broke his neck, and died. He had been a judge in Israel for forty years.

110. RETURN OF THE ARK

1 Samuel 5 - 6

When the Philistines arrived back home with the ark, they took it to the house where their god, Dagon, was kept. They set the ark of the covenant beside the idol and left it for the night.

The next day, the statue had fallen over again. Dagon's head and hands were cut off and only the body of the idol remained.

People in the city started becoming ill by the hundreds. Soon the Philistines decided to send the ark back. They put it on a cart pulled by two cows.

"If the cows pull the cart in the direction of Israel, we will know that God brought all this sickness upon us," they said. "If the cows go the other way, we will know it happened by chance."

They let the cows loose and watched as they headed straight down the highway, carrying the ark back to Israel.

111. A KING FOR ISRAEL

1 Samuel 7 - 8

Samuel had been a great leader for the Israelite people. When he got too old to handle all the problems and needs of the people, he appointed his two sons as judges. Samuel's sons were not wise and faithful like their father. It wasn't long before the Israelite people came to Samuel to complain about them.

"You are old and your sons are not good leaders like you were," they told him. "We want a king like all the other nations have."

Samuel didn't think much of the idea, but he went to ask the Lord for advice first.

"Give the people what they ask for," God said. "They are not rejecting you as their leader; they are rejecting me. If it is a king they want, they will have one. But warn them first about all that will happen to them if they are ruled by a king."

Samuel told the people that a king would treat them any way he pleased. He warned them that if they were unhappy with their new king, they were not to come crying to the Lord because he would not help them. Still the people insisted, so God told Samuel to find a king for the Israelites.

112. THE LOST DONKEYS

1 Samuel 9

A farm boy named Saul was helping his father one day in the field. His father asked him to take one of the servants and go look for two donkeys that were missing from the farm.

Saul did as his father asked. He and the servant traveled many miles but could find no trace of the animals. Saul was about to turn back when he remembered that a wise man of God named Samuel lived in the next city.

"Everything this man says comes true," Saul told the servant. "Perhaps he can tell us where to find the donkeys."

God had told Samuel that he would be sending him a young man to be made king of the people. When Saul arrived at Samuel's house, Samuel knew he was the one God had sent.

"Come and eat dinner with me," Samuel said to Saul. "You can spend the night here. And don't worry about your lost donkeys, they have been found."

Saul was surprised because he had not mentioned the donkeys to Samuel. He knew Samuel was a true prophet of God.

113. KING SAUL

1 Samuel 9 - 10

As Saul headed home the next day, Samuel walked with him.

"I have a secret that only you can hear," Samuel said. "God has called you to be the new king of Israel."

Saul could not believe what he was hearing. Then Samuel told him that three things would happen to him on the way home.

"If these three things come to pass, you will know that I am telling the truth," Samuel said. Everything happened just as Samuel had said.

Later, Samuel called the people together to announce who their new king would be. He asked Saul's tribe to come forward; then he pulled Saul's family out of that group. But when he looked for Saul, he discovered that Saul had run away to hide in the baggage.

The people went after Saul and brought him back. Everyone could see him standing in front because he was a tall man. They shouted, "Long live the king!"

Samuel told the people about the rules of the kingdom; then he sent everybody home, including the new King Saul.

114. SAUL LEADS A BATTLE

1 Samuel 11

An Ammonite army came to the Israelite city of Jabesh to start a battle with them. The people were afraid of the large Ammonite army, so they tried to make a peace treaty with them instead.

The Ammonite leader said to them, "I will make a treaty with you if you will let me put out the right eye of each of your citizens and send them as a message to Israel."

The people of Jabesh begged the Ammonites to give them seven days to look for someone to help them. Saul came home one day from the fields to find everyone in his house crying. When he heard about the Ammonites' threat, he was filled with the Spirit of God.

"Tell the Israelites to put together an army to help our people in Jabesh, or I will kill all their oxen," he said.

The Israelites sent over 300,000 soldiers. Saul led them to victory over the Ammonites. After that, all the people of Israel were ready to accept Saul as their king.

115. SAUL DISPLEASES GOD

1 Samuel 13

Saul had only been king for a short while when he began to take matters into his own hands. He became very proud when his son Jonathan defeated a small group of Philistines in a place called Geba. The Philistines pulled all their forces together, and soon their army numbered 30,000 chariots and 6,000 horsemen.

Saul waited for the prophet Samuel to come and tell him what to do next. He had promised to talk to Samuel first before he made any decisions. The Lord would speak to Samuel, and he would carry the message to Saul.

Saul waited almost a week for Samuel to arrive. Finally, he went ahead and made an offering to God himself. Samuel arrived as Saul was finishing with the offering.

"You have done a foolish thing, Saul," Samuel said to him. "Because you didn't follow God's rules, he will find another king to rule Israel. Your son Jonathan will never follow you on your throne."

116. A SURPRISE ATTACK

1 Samuel 13 - 14

Saul and his son, Jonathan, had only about 600 men in their army. But Jonathan was not happy just to sit around and wait for the Philistines to attack. He went to the soldier who carried the armor to ask if he would go with him to where the Philistines were camped.

The soldier agreed to go, and Jonathan told him his plan. "If the Philistines tell us to stay where we are, we will run before they can catch us. But if they tell us to come over to them, we will know that God is helping us."

When the two men reached the pass between the two camps, the Philistines told them to come on across. Jonathan and the soldier attacked the men who were guarding the entrance to the pass and killed twenty of them. Suddenly an earth tremor shook the ground beneath them, and the Philistines panicked.

Saul and his army came to find out what all the confusion was about. They saw the Philistines attacking each other in fright. The small Israelite army was able to chase the Philistines out of the country.

117. SAUL'S DISOBEDIENCE

1 Samuel 15 - 16

Saul led many other successful battles for the Israelites. Still, he did not keep God's commandments. He was more interested in the things he could gain after the battles than in killing those who worshiped idols.

The Lord told Samuel that a new king must be found, but the prophet did not want to replace Saul. He went to talk to him. "You give sacrifices to God to try and win him over," Samuel said to him. "Don't you know that obedience is more important to the Lord than sacrifice?"

It was no use; Saul would not follow God's law. Samuel went away and never saw Saul again. God told Samuel not to be sorry that he had made Saul king. It was time to appoint the new king God had chosen.

"Take a cow and go to Bethlehem to offer it as sacrifice," God said. "Invite Jesse, the son of Obed and grandson of Ruth, and all his sons to come. I will show you who is to be king."

118. ISRAEL'S SHEPHERD KING

1 Samuel 16

The prophet Samuel knew that one of Jesse's sons was to be the next king. He looked at each one in the house carefully. They all looked strong and brave, but God did not choose any of them.

"I don't look at people as you do," God said. "You can only see what is on the outside of a person, but I can see what is in the heart."

Finally Samuel asked Jesse if he had any more sons. Jesse sent for his youngest son, David, who was in the fields looking after the sheep.

When the boy walked through the door, God whispered to Samuel that he was the one. Samuel took the oil he had brought with him and poured some on David's head. At that very moment, the Spirit of God left King Saul and came upon David from that day forward.

119. A SONG FOR KING SAUL

1 Samuel 16

King Saul began to be troubled and mean. His servants came to him one day and offered to find someone to play the harp for him. One of the servants mentioned the son of a man called Jesse who could not only play the harp, but was also a brave warrior and a man of God.

"Bring me this man," said the king.

Soon afterward, David arrived, carrying gifts of food for the king on his donkey. Saul liked David from the first time he met him. Whenever the evil spirit came over Saul, he would call for David to come play his harp and make it go away.

After some time, Saul asked David to be his armor bearer when he went into battle so that David could always be at his side. Little did Saul know that the man who played the harp for him and carried his armor was the same man who would take his place as king.

120. GOLIATH'S CHALLENGE

1 Samuel 17

Another battle broke out between the Israelites and the Philistines. A big valley separated the two armies. One day the Philistines sent a soldier down from the hill where they camped into the valley to meet with the Israelites.

This soldier was not an ordinary man. He was many times bigger than the largest of the other soldiers. This giant, whose name was Goliath, wore enough armor on his body to crush an average man. His sword was so large that he carried it in both hands. Another soldier walked before him, carrying his shield.

"Why should we send our armies into battle?" Goliath said to the Israelites. "Choose a man to come out and fight me. If he can beat me, the Philistines will surrender to you. But if I beat him, you will all be our servants."

Saul and his men were afraid and didn't know how to answer the challenge. They had no one big enough to stand up to the giant. Little did they know that a young shepherd would come to their rescue.

121. BRAVE DAVID

1 Samuel 17

David's three older brothers had been called into battle, but David had stayed home to help his father with the sheep. Jesse had not heard from his elder sons for many days. He asked David to go to where the Israelites were fighting and take food to his brothers.

David arrived at the camp and started looking for his brothers. About that time, Goliath approached the camp. He yelled out his challenge again, and the men were so frightened that many of them ran off.

One of David's brothers saw him talking to the Israelite soldiers.

"What are you doing here?" he asked. "You should be home looking after the sheep."

"I haven't done anything wrong," said David. "That man has no right to come over here and make threats to God's army."

The soldiers told Saul what David had said. No one else had dared to say anything against the giant, so Saul wanted to meet the young man who talked so bravely.

122. A GIANT IS DEFEATED

1 Samuel 17

David came before Saul and said to him, "There is no reason for your men to be afraid. I will fight the Philistine."

"You can't fight that giant," King Saul said to him. "You are just a boy."

"God helped me kill the wild animals that attacked my father's sheep, and God will help me now," David said.

David had learned to use a sling as a weapon. He went down to the creek and found five stones to put in his shepherd's bag. Then he went out to meet the giant face to face.

"Come here," Goliath yelled. "I'll kill you and feed your flesh to the birds and the beasts."

"You have your sword and army," David said to him, "but I have the power of the Lord with me."

David took a stone from his bag, put it in the sling, and whirled it over his head. When he let it go, the stone hit Goliath in the middle of his forehead. The giant was dead!

123. THE KING FEARS DAVID

1 Samuel 17 - 18

King Saul was puzzled by all that had happened. A young shepherd boy had killed a giant with one small stone.

"Whose son is this?" he asked one of his servants.

When Saul found out that David was the same youth who had been able to chase his evil spirits away, he welcomed him back to his house. David became close friends with Jonathan, Saul's son, and Saul gave David an officer's rank in the army.

The women in the village came out to greet their new hero. They sang and danced to a special song: "Saul has killed thousands, and David has killed ten thousands."

From that day on, Saul became very jealous of David. He made up his mind to get rid of David as soon as possible. He called for David to come in to play his harp. Saul hid a spear where David could not see it. When he thought David was not looking, he threw it at him.

But God was with David, and he jumped out of the way just in time. Saul tried to stab David again, and again the Lord saved him. Then Saul decided the only way he could get rid of David was to send him to fight the Philistines and hope they killed him.

124. A TRUE FRIEND

1 Samuel 19

Saul called his son and their servants together one day. He told them it was time that they got rid of David once and for all. Jonathan was very sad to hear his father's words because he loved David like a brother.

"You must go and hide somewhere," Jonathan said to David. "My father has said that he will kill you."

Then Jonathan went back to try to make his father be reasonable. He reminded Saul that David had saved the Israelites by killing the great giant, Goliath. Saul promised his son that he would not harm David. But an evil spirit came again to Saul. When David returned from battle, Saul called for him to come in and play the harp. Saul had his spear ready, and once again, he tried to stab David with it.

David escaped to his house where his wife Michal told him that Saul planned to kill him the next day. Michal helped her husband escape. David went to see his old friend, the prophet Samuel.

125. A WARNING SIGNAL

1 Samuel 20

Soon David returned to ask Jonathan why his father wanted to kill him. Jonathan could not believe that Saul was really serious about going through with his threats.

"My father doesn't do anything without telling me," he said to David. "If you are so convinced that he plans to harm you, I will speak to him."

Jonathan told David to hide in the fields.

"The feast of the new moon is tomorrow night. I will talk to him then and find out how he feels about you," Jonathan said. "Then the next day I will go out to the field with my bow and arrow and shoot three arrows. If I say to the servant who is with me, 'The arrow is in front of you,' you will know it is safe to come out. But if I say, 'The arrow is farther out,' that will be a warning. The Lord is sending you away."

126. A SAD FAREWELL

1 Samuel 20

The next evening, Saul noticed that David was not at the feast table.

"He has gone to Bethlehem," Jonathan said to Saul. "He asked me to let him go be with his family to offer a sacrifice."

Saul was so mad that he began to scream at his servants to go get David and bring him back to be killed. Jonathan tried to stop his father, but when he did, Saul threw a spear at him!

Jonathan went out to the fields to give David the message that he should get as far away from Saul as possible. He shot the arrows, then sent his servant home so he could see David one last time. They were very sad because both David and Jonathan knew that David must leave and never come back again.

"May the Lord be with us always," Jonathan said, and he turned sadly for home.

127. DAVID TELLS A LIE

1 Samuel 21

David traveled to Nob to ask the priests there for food. Ahimelech was the High Priest. He came out to meet David, but he was afraid when he saw David was there alone.

David didn't want to make the priest suspicious. He told him that Saul had sent him on a secret mission.

"Do you have any bread?" David asked the priest.

Ahimelech said that the only bread in the temple was the sacred bread kept for the priests. David talked him into giving that bread to him, then he asked if there might be any weapons in the temple.

"We have the sword of Goliath," Ahimelech said to him.

David asked for that sword, and the priest gave it to him. He felt pretty clever getting Ahimelech to give him food and a weapon. However, David would soon be punished for lying.

128. DEATH OF THE PRIESTS

1 Samuel 22

Back at the palace, Saul was getting madder by the minute because no one could tell him where David had gone. A servant named Doeg was sitting in the back of the room.

"I saw Jesse's son, David, with Ahimelech the priest just the other day," Doeg told King Saul. "Ahimelech gave him food and a sword that belonged to Goliath the Philistine."

Saul flew into a rage when he heard about the sword. He ordered his men to go the shrine of Nob and bring Ahimelech and the other priests to him.

"Why did you give food and weapons to my enemy?" Saul asked Ahimelech.

Ahimelech told the king what David had said to him about being on a special errand. "I didn't know he was your enemy," Ahimelech said. "I thought he was your trusted son-in-law."

King Saul was very angry that David had been able to fool the priest and escape. He ordered his men to kill all the priests. The king had gone crazy with his anger and jealousy.

129. SAUL LOOKS FOR DAVID

1 Samuel 23

David heard that the Philistines had captured a city called Keilah. He had about 600 men in his army, but they were afraid to attack the Philistines and take back the city.

David spoke to the Lord to ask what he should do. God told him to attack and to trust in the Lord's presence. So David and his men marched in and defeated the Philistines.

Saul heard of David's victory. He was determined to catch David while he was still within the city walls of Keilah. God told David that he was in danger. He took his men and fled to some caves in a nearby hill. Word soon got to Saul about David's plans and the chase was on.

The men in David's camp wanted him to kill Saul and be done with him. David knew that would not be right. God had made Saul king of the Israelites. It was not yet time for David to take over the throne.

130. SAUL'S ROBE

1 Samuel 24

Once Saul came to the place where David and his men were hiding. He walked in the door of one of the caves and sat down to rest his feet. David was hiding in the back of the cave with his men.

"Kill him," the men whispered.

David refused to harm the king, but he could not resist doing a little mischief. He got close enough to the king to cut off a little piece of his robe. Saul got up to leave, and David ran after him. When Saul looked around, David bowed before him.

"What makes you think I want to hurt you?" David asked him. "The Lord brought you close enough to me that I could have killed you, but I would not."

David showed him the piece of his robe. The king was surprised. Once again David had gotten the better of him.

"You are more righteous than I am," Saul said to him. "I know that someday the Lord will make you the king of Israel. Just promise me that you will always be good to my family."

131. A SELFISH MAN

1 Samuel 25

David and his men wandered through the land seeking food and shelter. They came to some fields owned by a rich man called Nabal.

"We wish to live in peace with you and help look after your fields," they said to him. "If you would share with us the food you give your other servants, we would appreciate it very much."

Nabal was a mean man. He certainly didn't want to share his servants' food with a bunch of wandering outcasts. Nabal's selfishness made David angry. He gathered his men to attack Nabal's fields. One of Nabal's shepherds heard that David was on his way and went to warn Nabal's wife, Abigail.

Abigail knew she must do something to make up for her husband's meanness. So she packed plenty of food for all of David's men. Her servants loaded the baskets onto their donkeys and set off to meet David. Then she followed them.

132. THE GOOD WIFE

1 Samuel 25

When Abigail saw David, she got off her donkey and bowed on the ground before him.

"Please don't punish us for my husband's foolish behavior," she said. "I have brought food and gifts for your men. Take them and go in peace."

Then Abigail spoke to David about the Lord's plan for him to become the king of Israel. David knew that she must be a good and righteous woman to know of such things.

"Thank you for coming out here to talk to me," David said to her. "I will take your good advice."

Abigail returned home and found a big feast going on. Nabal and his men had been eating and drinking all the time she had been gone.

When Nabal awoke from his drunkenness, Abigail told him how his selfishness had nearly cost them their lives. Nabal was so upset that he became ill and died ten days later.

133. THE KING'S SPEAR

1 Samuel 26

Saul gathered 3,000 Israelite soldiers to chase David again. David sent spies to find out where Saul's tent was located. One evening he asked for a volunteer to go down to the camp with him. His nephew Abishai said he would go.

The two of them sneaked into Saul's camp that night while everyone was asleep. They found Saul lying asleep in a trench. His guard, Abner, and some other soldiers lay around him. Abishai spotted a spear that was stuck in the ground right next to Saul.

"Look!" he said to David. "God has delivered your enemy right into your hands. Let me finish him off with the spear."

"No," David said. "The Lord made him king, and the Lord will deal with him when the time comes."

So instead, they took the spear and a bottle of water while no one was looking. When they were a good distance from the camp, David yelled to Abner: "I thought you were supposed to be the best man in the land. You can't even protect your own king. Look where his spear and water bottle are now!"

134. SAMUEL'S SPIRIT

1 Samuel 27 - 28

In order to get away from Saul, David went to the Philistine land of Achish. He asked the leader if he could seek shelter in his land and told him he would help fight against Israel.

Saul was afraid when he saw the Philistine army waiting to attack him. He called to the Lord for help. When no answer came, he knew that God was no longer with him. No one but the prophet Samuel had ever been able to help Saul hear God's word, but Samuel had died.

"Find someone who can talk to the spirits of the dead," Saul said to his servants. They found a woman claiming to have such powers near the Israelite border. She called Samuel's spirit to come and talk to Saul.

"The Philistines have come to attack us," Saul cried to the spirit. "God will no longer talk to me. I don't know what to do."

"If the Lord has left you, there is nothing I can do for you," Samuel's spirit replied. "You have disobeyed God, and tomorrow he will send you and your sons up to be with me!"

135. MISSING FAMILIES

1 Samuel 29 - 30

The Philistines prepared to march against King Saul and the Israelites. Because David had joined Achish and his men, he was expected to fight. Not all of the Philistine soldiers trusted David as Achish did. They demanded that David and his men be sent back to Ziklag with their families.

David was glad to be sent back. He didn't really want to fight against the Israelites. He and his men traveled for three days to Ziklag, but when they arrived, they found that an army of the Amalekites had destroyed everything. None of the women and children could be found. David called on the Lord to tell him what he should do next.

"Go after them," God told him. "You can defeat them and take back what is yours."

136. DAVID IN BATTLE

1 Samuel 30

David took four hundred of his men with him to fight the Amalekites. When they found the army, they were dancing and drinking to celebrate their victory. David's men attacked them and fought until all but four hundred of the Amalekite soldiers lay dead.

All that had been taken was recovered. After they had rested, the men started on their journey back to Ziklag. Two hundred members of David's army had stayed behind because they were too weak from lack of food and sleep.

"We shouldn't have to share what we've won with them," the soldiers said. "We did all the work."

But David reminded them that God had won the battle for them. "The ones who stayed with the supplies had just as big a part in the battle as the ones who fought it," he said. "All will share alike."

137. THE DEATH OF SAUL

1 Samuel 31

The Philistine soldiers marched against Saul and his men the day after Saul had heard the message from Samuel's spirit. The Israelite soldiers were defeated in the battle, and many of them were killed. Saul and his sons fled, but the Philistines chased them and killed Jonathan and his brothers.

An arrow struck Saul, and he lay wounded on the ground. He begged his armor-bearer to kill him before the Philistines found him and tortured him. The man was unable to do the thing his master had asked. Saul then took his sword and fell down upon it, killing himself.

Philistine soldiers found the dead bodies of Saul and his sons. They cut off their heads and stripped them of their armor to show the Philistine people that they had conquered the Israelite leader.

That night the brave men of Israel went to find Saul's body. They took his bones to a sacred place and buried them under a tamarisk tree.

138. JOAB AND ABNER

2 Samuel 2 - 4

God told David to return to the Israelite city of Hebron. The men of Judah came to him and made him the king of their people. David asked the Lord to bless the people and make them strong.

Saul's guard, Abner, had escaped the battle that had taken the life of his master. He was able to save Saul's son, Ish-Bosheth, and together they traveled to another part of Israel where Abner appointed Ish-Bosheth the king.

The army of David and the army of Ish-Bosheth fought many battles. Abner was the general of Ish-Bosheth's forces. He and David's general, Joab, became great enemies.

Abner realized he was on the losing side. He promised David he would bring the army of Ish-Bosheth to unite with his army.

Joab was not pleased when he heard what Abner had said. He took Abner aside and killed him. Some of Ish-Bosheth's men heard about Abner's death and decided to kill Ish-Bosheth. They brought his head to David, thinking they would be rewarded. Instead, David had the two men killed as punishment for murdering Saul's son.

139. DAVID THE KING

2 Samuel 5 - 6

The leaders of the tribes of Israel came to meet with David. "We are all Israelites of the same flesh and blood," they said. "The Lord has said that you will lead our people."

Then they made David king of Israel. The first thing he did was to go to the city of Jerusalem to claim it as his city. The Jebusites who lived in Jerusalem did not fear David and his men because they had built great walls around the city to protect it from attacks.

David told his men that any one of them who could climb up the gutters on the side of the walls and get into the city would be the new captain of the army. His men came forward and went over the walls and defeated the Jebusites. Jerusalem was then known as the city of David.

Soon the Philistines heard that David had been made the king of Israel. They sent armies to battle with him. With God's help, David was able to defeat them.

140. THE ARK IS HOME

2 Samuel 6

David took 30,000 men with him to bring the ark of the covenant from Judah to the city of David. Two men, Uzzah and Ahio, were to drive the cart carrying the ark. The oxen at the front of the cart stumbled, and Uzzah grabbed the ark to keep it from falling off. But no one was to touch the ark of the covenant, and God punished Uzzah. When David saw that his servant lay dead, he was afraid and decided to leave the ark at the house of a man named Obed-Edom.

One day a message came to David from Obed-Edom. He said that everyone in the house had been blessed because of the ark. Then David knew that the time had come to bring the ark back to Jerusalem.

The people who made the trip with David were filled with joy. They danced and sang and blew their trumpets. David stopped many times along the way to offer sacrifices to God to thank him for his blessing. The group entered the city of Jerusalem, still dancing with all their might.

141. THANKING GOD

2 Samuel 6

David's wife, Michal, who was Saul's daughter, looked out her window and saw David leaping and singing along with the people. Her heart filled with hatred for him because she thought a king should not behave like that.

David gave every person in the city some bread, a piece of meat, and some wine before he sent them to their houses. Then he went home to share his blessings with his own family. Michal came out to meet him.

"You weren't acting like a king today," she said. "You showed yourself in front of the whole city. Now they will have no respect for you at all."

"It is not for the people that I danced and played. It was for the Lord who made me king of Israel instead of your brothers," David said to her. "And I will continue to show my thanks to him forever."

142. A HOUSE FOR THE LORD

2 Samuel 7

For the first time in many years, the Israelites were at peace. David sat in his beautiful house made of the finest cedar and thought of the wonderful things God had done for him.

David called for Nathan the prophet one day.

"It is not fair that I live in a beautiful house while the ark of God still sits in a tent," David said to him.

Nathan urged David to go ahead with his plans to build a house for God's ark. That night God visited Nathan.

"Tell David that it is not time to build a permanent home for the ark. I have traveled with the people of Israel since I brought them out of Egypt." God said to Nathan. "I will give my people a place where they will never have to move again."

Nathan brought the message of God to David.

"It is not you who will build the house of the Lord, but one of your sons," Nathan said. "God will make your son a king, and his kingdom will rule forever."

143. PROMISE OF KINDNESS

2 Samuel 9

Before Jonathan was killed, David had promised him that he would take care of Jonathan's family after he became king. David wanted to keep his promise, but it seemed that everyone in Jonathan's family had been killed.

One of Saul's former servants was brought to David. The servant, whose name was Ziba, said to King David, "There is one grandson of Saul's named Mephibosheth who still lives."

When David's men brought Mephibosheth before the king, he dropped to the floor in fear.

"Don't be afraid of me," David said to him. "I didn't bring you here to harm you; I want to give you back the land that was taken from Saul."

"Why would you do this for me?" he asked.

"I do this for Jonathan's sake," David replied. "I will send Ziba and some men out to Saul's land to care for the field, but you are welcome to stay here in the place with me."

144. DAVID BREAKS A LAW

2 Samuel 11

The Israelites were at war again, this time with the Ammonites. David usually led the army himself, but he sent Joab and stayed home instead.

David lay on his bed one evening, but he couldn't rest. He got up to go out on his rooftop and look around the city. David could see a woman who was bathing herself. He looked at her for a long time, admiring her beauty. Then he sent one of his servants to find out who she was.

"She is Bathsheba," the servant told him. "She is married to one of your soldiers, Uriah."

David forgot about God's law against adultery. He wanted Bathsheba even though she was someone else's wife. He sent messengers for her, and took her to his home.

Later, David received word from Bathsheba that she was expecting a baby. He knew people would learn of his sin since Uriah had been away fighting the war. So he sent a message to his general Joab to have Uriah return home at once.

145. URIAH DIES

2 Samuel 11

When Uriah returned, David asked him a few questions about the battles, then told him to go home for a few days. The next morning, David was upset to find that Uriah had spent the night outside the door of the palace.

"I can't go home to my comforts while the rest of the army is sleeping in tents," Uriah said to the king.

David decided he needed another plan to hide the sin he had committed.

The next day David wrote a letter and gave it to Uriah to deliver to Joab. Uriah had no idea that the letter was about his own death.

"Put Uriah at the front of the battle," David wrote to Joab. "Then pull back your soldiers so that Uriah will be killed."

Joab obeyed the king's orders. He told his best men to go to the front of the line, and Uriah went with them. Many men died along with Uriah.

146. DAVID AND BATHSHEBA

2 Samuel 11

A messenger arrived at the palace with news of the battle. "The soldiers came close to the gates of the Ammonite city," he told David. "The enemy shot at them from over the wall. Many of your soldiers are dead. Your servant, Uriah, is dead, too."

"Tell Joab not to be discouraged," David said to the messenger. "The sword kills one man as easily as it does another. Tell him to fight harder next time."

Bathsheba was sad at the news of her husband's death. David waited until she had mourned for Uriah for a decent time. Then he brought her back to the palace and married her. A baby son was born to them soon after.

What David had done was wrong in the eyes of God. Even though David was king, he had displeased God.

147. THE STORY OF A LAMB

2 Samuel 12

G od sent Nathan the prophet to tell David a story. "There were two men who lived in the city. One man was rich and the other was very poor. The poor man had nothing but a little baby lamb that he had taken care of since its birth.

"Once the rich man had a visitor and wanted to make a feast for the traveler, but instead of taking a sheep from one of his own herds, he took the poor man's young lamb."

Nathan's story made David angry. "That man deserves to

die for doing such a terrible thing," he said. "He should be made to give the poor man four of his sheep to replace the one lamb."

Then Nathan said to David, "You are that man! You had everything you could ever want; yet you took Uriah's wife."

"You are right," said David. "I have sinned against God."

"God has forgiven you," Nathan said. "You will not die, but the son you have with Bathsheba will be taken from you."

148. ABSALOM

2 Samuel 12 - 13

After Nathan left the palace, Bathsheba's baby became very sick. For seven days, David prayed and fasted for his son, but he could not be saved.

Bathsheba soon gave David another son they named Solomon. Solomon had many half-brothers and sisters because David had taken several different wives over the years, as was the custom in that time.

Amnon was the oldest of David's sons. He tricked his half-sister, Tamar, into coming to his house one day. When he was cruel to her, her full brother, Absalom, vowed to get back at Amnon for what he had done.

Two years passed before Absalom got his revenge. He went to his father, David, and begged him to let Amnon go with him to a feast. When the king agreed, Absalom gave his servant instructions to get Amnon drunk and then kill him.

A servant came to David and told him that his son Amnon was dead. Absalom knew his father would be angry so he stayed away for three years to keep David from punishing him.

149. JOAB'S PLAN

2 Samuel 14

Joab could tell that the king missed seeing his son, Absalom. He thought of a plan to bring father and son back together. Joab knew a woman who was good at acting out stories. He sent her to visit the king.

"I am a widow," she said to David. "I had two sons, but there was a terrible fight between them. One son killed the other one, and now my family wants me to surrender my only living son so they can kill him in revenge."

"Go back to your house," David said to her. "I will see that nothing happens to your son."

The woman hesitated, so the king asked if there was something else she wanted to say.

"You have been so good as to ask for mercy for my son," she said. "Shouldn't you also grant the same mercy for your own son?"

Joab stood nearby.

"Bring Absalom back," David told Joab. "But let him live in his own house and not set eyes on me."

150. ABSALOM RETURNS

2 Samuel 15

Once he was back in the king's good graces, Absalom prepared to take over the throne that he felt was his rightful inheritance. He brought together fifty men with their chariots and horses. Then he sent spies to the land of Hebron where David had first been named king.

"When you hear trumpets sound," he said to them, "say that Absalom is now the king of Hebron."

Then Absalom told David he had to go back to Hebron to fulfill a promise he had made to God. David told him to go in peace, so Absalom set off with two hundred of David's unsuspecting soldiers.

Not long after Absalom left, a messenger told David that many people wanted Absalom to take over his throne.

"Prepare to leave Jerusalem at once," David told all his servants.

Six hundred soldiers left the city with David. He told Zadok and Abithar, the priests, to stay in Jerusalem.

"You must tell me when it is time for me to return," he told them. "If the Lord allows, I will come again to the city to worship and live."

151. DAVID FLEES

2 Samuel 16

David and his men traveled to the Mount of Olives where they met Hushai, a loyal friend and advisor. Hushai wanted to go with David, but David had another plan.

"You can help me more if you go back to Jerusalem," David told him. "Convince Absalom that you no longer follow me. When you have won his trust, send news of his plan to me through Zadok and Abiathar. Their young sons will come out to find me."

A man from the house of Saul saw David and his men approaching the town where he lived. He ran out and began cursing David and throwing stones at him.

"Why do you let this man get away with this?" the king's soldiers asked. "Let us kill him for you."

But David would not let his men harm the man. He told them that the Lord had sent the man to curse him for his sins.

152. TWO MESSENGERS

2 Samuel 17

Absalom's adviser wanted him to attack David immediately. He knew that David's group would be disorganized because they had left the city so quickly.

"Let me choose 12,000 men and go after David tonight," the adviser said.

Absalom liked the plan. At the last minute, he decided to ask Hushai for his advice. Since Hushai had once been so close to David, he might have a better idea.

"If you attack David now, it will be a slaughter," Hushai told Absalom. "It would be better to wait and lead the battle yourself. That way you will get all the credit."

Absalom took Hushai's advice. Then Hushai slipped a message to the priests Zadok and Abiathar, and they sent a note to David by their sons, Jonathan and Ahimaaz, as they had planned. David would be ready for Absalom's next move.

153. HANGING BY A HAIR

2 Samuel 18

David prepared his soldiers to fight. He divided them into groups of hundreds and groups of thousands and assigned generals to each group. David planned to lead his army, but his men convinced him to stay behind where he would be safe.

Before they went out to meet Absalom and his army, David gave his general, Joab, one last request. When they found Absalom, he was to be treated with fairness and kindness.

The two armies met in a forest in Ephraim. Joab led the Israelite army into battle because the men had convinced David that he should stay behind where he would be safe. Twenty thousand men died in the fighting, but Joab was able to claim victory.

Absalom happened to meet some of David's soldiers after the battle. He tried to ride away, but his long hair got caught in the branches of a big oak tree. The donkey he was riding kept on going, and Absalom was left hanging by his hair. He lost his life trying to revolt against his father, King David.

154. ABSALOM IS KILLED

2 Samuel 18

One of the soldiers saw what had happened to Absalom. He remembered David had told them to be good to his son, so he left Absalom hanging in the tree instead of capturing him. When the soldier told Joab, the general replied, "If you saw him, why didn't you just go ahead and kill him? I would have paid you a large reward for getting rid of Absalom."

The soldier reminded Joab about the king's request, but Joab didn't stay to listen. He was already going to the woods to find Absalom and kill him.

The armies were still fighting when they heard the sound of a trumpet. Joab blew on the instrument with great force to let the people know that Absalom was dead and the war was over.

Ahimaaz, the son of Zadok, the priest, asked Joab if he could run and tell King David the news of the victory right away. But Joab knew the king would not want to hear about the death of Absalom. Finally he gave a message to another man to take to David. A little later Joab let Ahimaaz go also.

155. KING DAVID RETURNS

2 Samuel 18 - 19

David had returned to the gates of the city to wait for his men to bring news of the fighting. Ahimaaz arrived first.

"All is well," he said to the King. "The Lord has blessed you this day and saved you from your enemies."

But Ahimaaz pretended not to know about Absalom. When the other messenger arrived, David asked if he knew what happened to Absalom.

"All of your enemies should end up as he did," the man said.

David knew by the man's comment that his son had been killed. He began to cry, and turned away. "Oh, Absalom!" he said. "I wish it had been me instead of you!"

The people saw how deeply hurt the king was by his son's death. Instead of being happy about their victory, they felt ashamed. Joab came to talk to David.

"These people saved our life, and now you make them feel ashamed," he said. "You act as if you wish we had all died instead of Absalom."

119

So the king came out again to greet his soldiers, and the people of Israel sent word that they were ready to accept David back in Jerusalem.

156. A NEW KING

1 Kings 1

As David grew older, his oldest son Adonijah decided to take over his father's throne. He chose fifty men to follow him and began to prepare a feast for his coronation.

Zadok the priest and Nathan the prophet heard about Adonijah's plans. They knew King David wanted his son Solomon to be the next king. Since no one had invited them to the feast, Nathan and Zadok thought Adonijah must be planning to take over the throne behind his father's back. They went to Bathsheba to warn her of Adonijah's plans.

"You must go to the king and tell him what is going on," they told her.

When Bathsheba told David the whole story, he gave orders to Zadok and Nathan to bring Solomon right away.

"Take him to Gihon and anoint him with oil," David told them. "Then blow the trumpet and shout, 'God save King Solomon.' He will sit on my throne."

157. SOLOMON AND ADONIJAH

1 Kings 2

Adonijah and his followers were having their feast when word came of Solomon's coronation. Adonijah left for the tabernacle because he was afraid of what Solomon might do. He grabbed the horns of the altar, hoping he would be safe.

Solomon's voice spoke to Adonijah.

"Don't fear me," the voice said. "If you prove to be an honest and worthy man, I promise I will never let anything happen to you. But if you start doing bad things, you will die."

After David's death, Solomon sat on his throne. One day Adonijah asked Bathsheba to go to Solomon to ask a favor for him. He wanted to marry King David's former nurse, Abishag. When Bathsheba asked Solomon if the marriage could take place, the king flew into a rage. He ordered Adonijah to be killed that day.

158. WISE SOLOMON

1 Kings 3

O ne night King Solomon had a dream in which God spoke to him. "I will grant you a wise and understanding heart," the Lord said to him. Then God told him that he would give him many riches, also.

When Solomon awoke from his dream, he was very grateful to God. He went to the ark of the covenant to offer a sacrifice. Two women came before him and asked him to settle their argument. The women had both had babies, but one of the babies had died.

"That woman stole my baby in the night," one of them said. "Her baby is dead."

The other woman argued that the baby belonged to her and that no switch had taken place. Solomon asked that a sword be brought to him.

"We'll divide the living child in two and give each of you half," he said.

One of the women screamed, "Please don't hurt him. I'd rather let her have him than see him killed."

Solomon wisely gave the child to the woman who spoke up because he knew she was the baby's real mother.

159. GOD'S HOUSE

1 Kings 5, 6, 8

Solomon set out to build the great temple that David had wanted. He sent for help to a king named Hiram who had been a close friend of King David's.

Solomon asked for Hiram's help in cutting the cedar trees growing in Lebanon. Soon the materials began to arrive for the new building. Solomon brought in 3,300 people to work on the temple. They carried the huge stones and pieces of timber and started putting up the walls of God's house.

When the outside was finished, Solomon had the inside covered with gold. It took seven years to build the walls and ceilings of the temple. When they were through, the king ordered the ark of the convenant to be put inside it.

All the people of Israel gathered to welcome the ark into its new home. After the priests took the ark inside the temple, a cloud filled the temple and the people knew that God's spirit was with them.

160. SOLOMON'S RICHES

1 Kings 7, 9, 10

After the building was completed, God came to speak to Solomon again. "I am pleased with all you have done, Solomon," God said to him. "If you will always follow me and keep my commandments, then I will bless your kingdom forever. But if you turn away from me, I will send evil to this house and its people."

From that day, Solomon's power increased over the land. The Queen of Sheba heard about the famous King Solomon and decided to pay him a visit. She had many hard questions to ask him to test his wisdom.

Solomon welcomed the queen to his home. He answered all her questions, and she was very impressed.

"Everything I heard about you is true," she said. "Your wisdom is as great as your kingdom."

Then she gave him the spices, gold, and jewels she had brought with her, and he told her to take anything of his that she desired. The queen thanked him for his generosity and returned home with her servants.

161. TEMPLES FOR IDOLS

1 Kings 11

King Solomon was wise in many ways, yet he showed little wisdom when it came to the women he chose to marry. He took the daughter of the Pharaoh of Egypt to be his wife. He also married women from tribes who worshiped idols.

He wanted his wives to be happy, so he built temples for their idols. Before long he began to worship the idols himself. The Lord became very angry with Solomon because he had turned his heart away from God.

"You have not kept my commandments as you promised to," God said to Solomon. "Now I will take your kingdom away from you. Because your father, David, was a loyal servant to me, I will not take away your throne, but I will see that your son doesn't keep it. He will have only one tribe left on his side. The rest of Israel will turn against him."

The nation of Israel would have to face war once again.

162. ISRAEL DIVIDED

1 Kings 11

A prophet named Ahijah came out to Jerusalem one day. He was looking for a young man named Jeroboam, who was one of the king's leaders. When he found Jeroboam, he took off the new coat he was wearing and ripped it into twelve pieces.

He handed ten pieces to Jeroboam and said to him: "The God of Israel has said that he will take the throne away from Solomon and give ten tribes to you."

King Solomon had been Israel's ruler for forty years when he died. His son, Rehoboam, was appointed to be the next king. But the people sent for Jeroboam and asked him to go with them to talk to the new king.

"We want to ask King Rehoboam to go easier on us than his father did," the people said. King Solomon had made the people work long hours to build his kingdom. They hoped his son would treat them better.

163. A STRONG LEADER

1 Kings 12

"Give me three days to think about what you have asked," King Rehoboam told Jeroboam and the people when they came to him. The king wanted to check with his advisers before he made a decision.

First, he went to ask the older men their opinion.

"If you will be fair with these people," they said, "they will be your loyal servants for life."

Then the king went to the young men of his age and asked what they would do.

"If you are too easy on these people, they will believe that your father was a stronger leader than you," the young men told him. "Go and tell them that you are going to be twice as hard on them as your father was."

King Rehoboam thought the young men had a good point. He didn't want to be known as a weak leader. When the people came back on the third day, he answered them, saying that he would make things even harder for them than before.

This was the reason the great kingdom of Solomon was divided into two kingdoms.

164. THE GOLDEN CALVES

1 Kings 12

The people of Israel were very angry with the king's answer. All of them but the tribe of Judah wanted Jeroboam to take over as king. In time, the country of Israel was divided as the prophet, Ahijah, had predicted. Jeroboam ruled ten tribes in Israel and Rehoboam ruled only one.

Jeroboam didn't want his people to have anything to do with Rehoboam's tribe in Judah. Each year when his people went back to worship in the temple that Solomon had built, he was afraid they would stay there and not come back. So Jeroboam made two golden calves and put them in different places for the people to worship.

"It's too far for you to go to Jerusalem every year," he told them. "These calves represent the gods who brought you out of Egypt."

Then Jeroboam appointed new priests of his own choosing and built temples for the people to worship in. In this way Jeroboam led the people to sacrifice to idols. They were not worshiping God.

165. THE ALTAR DESTROYED

1 Kings 13

One day a man of God came to the altar of the golden calves. He began to cry out that the Lord was sending a man who would one day destroy the priests who led the people in the worship of idols.

"As a sign that I am telling the truth, the Lord will cause this altar to break open and the ashes to fall out," the man said.

Jeroboam heard the man, and he reached out to grab him away from the altar. When he did, the king's arm would not move. He watched in horror as the altar split open, and ashes spilled out onto the ground.

Jeroboam knew that the man at the altar was a true prophet from God. He asked the man to pray for him and to take away the paralysis in his arm, and the man did.

"I want to reward you for healing my arm," the king said to him. "Please come home and have dinner with me."

But the man told him God had said that he must not eat or drink anything, and that he was to take a different route home.

166. THE PROPHET DISOBEYS

1 Kings 13

Another prophet who lived nearby heard all that happened at the altar of the calves that day, and he went out to meet the man on the road.

"Are you the man of God from Judah?" the prophet asked.

The man answered that he was, and the prophet asked him to come home and eat with him. The man told the prophet the same thing he had told the king about his orders from God.

"I am also a prophet," the other man said. "An angel of God told me I was supposed to bring you to my home to eat and drink with me."

The man didn't hold to his instructions from God that time. He went back with the other prophet and shared his dinner. While they were eating, God spoke to the man who had disobeyed through the other prophet.

"You didn't do as the Lord asked," he said. "Now when you die, you will be buried in a place far away from your family."

On his way home, the man was attacked and killed by a lion. Some men found his body and told the prophet about it.

He took the body of the man and buried it in his own family's burial place, which was a long distance from the man's home.

167. JEROBOAM'S PUNISHMENT

1 Kings 14

One of Jeroboam's sons became very sick one day. Jeroboam called for his wife and told her to go for help.

"Put on old clothes so you won't be recognized," he said. "Go to Shiloh and find the priest, Ahijah. Ask him what is going to happen to the little boy."

The servants packed up food and gifts for Jeroboam's wife to take with her to the priest.

Ahijah was a very old man. His eyesight was nearly gone. Still God spoke to him, and when the wife of Jeroboam walked through the door, Ahijah knew who she was.

"Come in," he told her. "It is no use to try and disguise yourself. I have some very bad news for you and your husband."

Ahijah told her that because Jeroboam had sinned against God by worshiping the idols, their son would not live.

"God will allow him to be buried," Ahijah said. "But a great evil will come over the house of Jeroboam, and the rest of your family will face a terrible death."

168. EVIL KINGS

1 Kings 15 - 16

After the deaths of Jeroboam and Rehoboam, many men tried to take over the throne of Israel. Rehoboam's son,

Abijam, became the king of Judah. Abijam worshiped idols just as his father had done. The only reason God let him become king was because of his great grandfather, David, who had been loyal to the Lord.

Abijam died two years later. When his son Asa became king, he destroyed the idols, but his mother kept one in a grove where she worshiped it. Asa found out about it, and told her she could not be queen anymore because she did not follow God.

Jeroboam's son, Nadab, ruled the rest of Israel for two years before a man named Baasha killed him and became the new leader. He had all of Jeroboam's family killed. As the prophet Ahijah had predicted, Baasha left the bodies lying in the streets and did not bury them. But Baasha did not follow God's commandments either. God sent word to him that his family would also one day lie dead in the streets.

169. SAMARIA

1 Kings 16

A man named Zimri led his army against Baasha and his men. He won the battle and destroyed all of Baasha's family. Omri had become the king of Judah. He knew that the people of Israel were frightened of Zimri, so he talked them into attacking Zimri at his palace. When Zimri saw that the people were against him, he set the palace on fire and killed himself before they could get to him.

Omri set up his palace in a place called Samaria. There he continued in the ways of the kings before him, building idols for his people to worship instead of following God's laws. After he died, his son Ahab became king. He married a woman named Jezebel who worshiped the idol Baal. Ahab built an altar to Baal in Samaria. That made God very angry, and a great punishment came upon the people.

170. A MESSAGE TO AHAB

1 Kings 17

A prophet of God named Elijah went to see Ahab one day. He had a message from God for the people who lived in Samaria and worshiped false idols.

"As the God of Israel lives," Elijah said to Ahab, "no rain or even dew will fall on this ground for many years to come."

Then God told Elijah to get away from the city and go to a brook near Cherith where God would look after him. Each day God sent ravens to Elijah, carrying food for him in their beaks. After the drought started and the brook dried up, God told Elijah to go the city of Zarephath and find a widow who would give him food and water.

When Elijah found the woman, he asked her for a drink of water, and she brought it to him. But when he asked for something to eat, she hesitated. "I have nothing baked and very little food in my house," she said.

"Don't be afraid," Elijah said to her. "Go bake your bread and bring the first piece to me. The Lord has said that you will not run out of wheat and oil for as long as the drought lasts."

171. THE WIDOW'S SON

1 Kings 17 - 18

While Elijah was staying with her, the woman's son got sick and died. Elijah was very upset that the Lord had allowed this bad thing to happen to the woman who had been so kind to him.

"Give me your son," Elijah said to her. He took the boy up on the roof and prayed to God for his life. God heard Elijah's prayer, and the boy came back to life.

Then Elijah brought the boy down into the house and said to the mother, "See, your son is alive." The boy's mother was very happy. She said to Elijah "Now I know for certain that you are a man of God, and that everything you say is true."

As Elijah had predicted, no rain or dew came to the country for three whole years. God told Elijah it was time for him to see King Ahab and put an end to the drought. So Elijah left the woman's house.

172. ELIJAH RETURNS

1 Kings 18

King Ahab called a man from his staff to help him look for grass near the riverbanks for the animals to eat. This man was named Obadiah and he believed in God.

Ahab told Obadiah to go one way to look for water while he went the other. Obadiah soon met Elijah walking down the road.

"Tell your king that Elijah is here," Elijah said.

"Why do you send me back to be killed?" Obadiah said.

131

"The king has looked for you all over this country but could not find you. What if I bring him here to see you and the Lord has taken you somewhere else? He will kill me for sure."

Elijah promised to stay where he was until Obadiah brought Ahab back. The king was furious with Elijah because he had predicted the terrible drought.

"Are you the one who has brought all the trouble to Israel?" Ahab asked.

"I haven't brought any trouble to Israel," Elijah answered. "You and your followers are the ones who broke God's commandments."

173. GOD SENDS PROOF

1 Kings 18

Elijah told Ahab to gather the people of Israel together and bring them to Mount Carmel. "Tell the four hundred fifty prophets of Baal to come and also the prophets who sit at Jezebel's table," Elijah told him.

King Ahab did as Elijah had asked. The people of Israel gathered with the false prophets on the mountain to see what Elijah had planned.

"How much longer are you people going to go on trying to follow two different gods?" Elijah said to them. "If the Lord is God, then follow him. But if Baal is the one, then follow him."

"I am the only prophet of God left," Elijah said. "There are four hundred fifty men of Baal here. Let us build two altars and place an offering on them, but do not set them on fire. You will call to Baal to send fire to your altar, and I will call on the name of the Lord to send fire to mine."

174. BAAL IS ASLEEP

1 Kings 18

The prophets of Baal built their altar and made it ready for the sacrifice. They began to call to Baal to send fire to the altar. For hours they prayed and shouted.

Elijah watched their efforts and began to make fun of them. "Your god must be doing something else," he said. "Or he could be asleep. You'd better yell very loud so you can wake him."

They shouted all day long, but still the altar was quiet. Elijah called for the people to come with him to an altar that had fallen apart. He repaired it as God instructed him; then he told the people to bring a lot of water to pour over it. Although water was very scarce, they did as he said and brought so much water that it filled a trench around the altar. The people were very curious to see what Elijah would do next.

175. FIRE IN THE ALTAR

1 Kings 18

Elijah began to pray before the altar: "Lord of Abraham, Isaac, and Israel," he said. "Let the people know that everything I have done was commanded by you so they will again believe in you as their God."

At that moment, fire shot out of the sky and lit up the sacrifice lying on the altar. It burned the wood and stones of the altar and even dried up the water in the trench.

When the people saw what had happened, they fell down and shouted, "The Lord is God! The Lord is God!"

"Go now and get something to eat and drink," Elijah said to Ahab. "Very soon the rain will begin to fall again on the earth."

Elijah took one of his servants with him to the top of Mount Carmel. He told him to go to the peak and look over at the ocean. The servant went up seven times before he spotted a small rain cloud coming from the ocean.

176. AN ANGRY QUEEN

1 Kings 19

Ahab was very excited by all he had seen that day on Mount Carmel. He told his wife Jezebel about the fire on the altar and the priests of Baal who had failed and been killed.

Queen Jezebel was outraged with Elijah. She sent a messenger to tell him that she intended to have the same thing done to him the next day.

Elijah decided he had better leave right away to escape the angry queen. He went into the desert where it was hot and dry, and he had no food or water.

By the end of the day he could go no farther. He sat down by a tree and began to wish that he could just die.

Soon he fell asleep. An angel touched him, and he heard a voice telling him to get up and eat. When he looked up, a cake of bread and some water sat in front of him. He ate and drank all of it and soon he was sound asleep again.

The angel came back and woke him a second time. "Get up now and eat because you need strength for your long journey."

177. ELIJAH WAITS

1 Kings 19

The meals from the angel gave Elijah the energy to travel for forty days and nights until he reached Mount Horeb. He found a cave there where he could wait for God to tell him what to do next.

God told Elijah to stand on the mountain while he passed by. Elijah watched as a great gust of wind blew by. The Lord wasn't in the wind though, so Elijah waited. Then an earthquake began to shake the ground below him, but God was not in the earthquake either. Elijah watched as a fire sprang up around him. Still, God was not present.

Then a small voice called to Elijah, asking him what he was doing there. Elijah knew that God was speaking to him. He told him again about his fears and disappointments with the people of Israel.

"This is what you must do," God told Elijah. "Go to Syria and appoint a man called Hazael to be king. Then you will anoint Jehu to be the new king of Israel. I will send you a helper named Elisha. There are seven thousand people left in Israel who still follow me. They will help you do what I have asked."

178. A BULLY KING

1 Kings 20

Ben-hadad was king of Syria during the days of King Ahab. He had a powerful army that he used to bully other nations into doing what he asked.

"Give me your women and children and all of your silver and gold," Ben-hadad said to King Ahab.

Ahab knew that his army was much smaller than the Syrian army. He didn't have a chance.

"Whatever I have is yours," he told Ben-hadad. So Ben-hadad sent a message that his servants would be there the next day to take whatever they wanted.

The people of Israel were not so ready to give up everything they treasured to this foreign king. So Ahab had to tell the Syrian king that he couldn't march into the city and take over.

Ben-hadad was not pleased with King Ahab's message. He vowed to turn the city of Samaria into a pile of dust.

179. SYRIA ATTACKS ISRAEL

1 Kings 20

A prophet came to Ahab to give him a message from the Lord. "God will deliver you from your enemies," he said. "Then you will know that he is the Lord of Israel."

Ben-hadad sat drinking in his royal tents. His men came to tell him that the Samarians were marching toward them. He told them to go easy on the Israelites because he didn't want to waste his men in battle on the small army.

Ahab led his servants out first to meet the Syrians. Then the seven thousand men in Israel's army followed behind and killed many of the surprised Syrian soldiers.

Ben-hadad tried to avenge his defeat the next year. This time the prophet told Ahab he must kill Ben-hadad. But after Ben-hadad was captured, he told Ahab he would give him some land if Ahab would let him go free. Ahab took his offer.

However, since he didn't do as God asked, it was to cost him his life.

180. NABOTH'S LAND

1 Kings 21

Next to King Ahab's palace was land owned by a man named Naboth. Naboth had a vineyard on the land where he raised grapes for fruit and wine.

One day Ahab went to Naboth and asked for the vineyard. "I want to plant a garden of herbs on the land," he said to him. "I will pay you a fair price for the land in money or with another vineyard."

"The Lord has told me not to give this land to you," Naboth said. "This land has been handed down from my father to me."

Ahab was very upset with Naboth's answer. He went to his room to lie down. Jezebel heard that the king refused to eat his supper. She went up to him to see what was the matter.

"Aren't you the king of Israel?" she said to him when he complained about Naboth. "Come down and eat. I will get Naboth's land for you."

181. NABOTH IS KILLED

1 Kings 21

Jezebel wrote letters to the elders of Samaria and signed Ahab's name to them. She ordered them to bring Naboth before the court where two men would testify that Naboth had cursed God and the king. Then they were to take him out and stone him to death.

After Jezebel's orders were carried out, she went to Ahab to tell him that Naboth was dead and the vineyard now belonged to him. Ahab rushed out to look over his new property and found Elijah the prophet waiting for him.

"The Lord will punish you for killing Naboth and taking his land," Elijah said to him. "You will end up dead in the street just as he did."

Ahab felt very sad for what he had done. He went back to the palace and fasted for many days. God told Elijah, "Ahab has become very humble before me. I will not bring evil now, but in his son's time, so that his house will be punished for his bad deeds."

182. AHAB'S FINAL BATTLE

1 Kings 22

Syria did not attack Israel again for three years. Ahab was pleased that he had been able to conquer the Syrians, not once but twice. He wanted the land of Ramoth because it had belonged to the Israelites. The king of Judah, Jehosphaphat, was visiting Ahab, and he asked Jehoshaphat to help him win the land back. Jehoshaphat thought they should see what the Lord had to say before they made any plans.

Four hundred of the king's prophets were brought together. They agreed that the Lord would being King Ahab victory.

"Aren't there any of the Lord's prophets here for us to talk to?" Jehoshaphat asked the king. He knew that the king's prophets only told him what he wanted to hear.

"There is one prophet called Micaiah who is a prophet of the Lord, but I hate to call on him. He never has anything good to say about me," King Ahab replied.

183. BAD NEWS FOR AHAB

1 Kings 22

Jehoshaphat insisted that Micaiah be brought before them. When he arrived, King Ahab asked him if they should go to war against Ramoth.

"The Lord will deliver the land of Ramoth into the hands of the king," Micaiah said to Ahab.

"How many times do I have to tell you?" Ahab said. "I want to hear the whole truth."

Micaiah told him of a vision he had of Israel's people scattered about like sheep without a shepherd. In the vision, the Lord told them to go home because they had no master.

"See there," Ahab said. "He has said that I will not return from battle. I told you he would give me bad news."

Ahab had Micaiah taken away to prison before he and Jehoshaphat left for the battle. The fighting had barely started when Ahab was struck with an arrow and killed. When the news spread that the king of Israel was dead, the soldiers left the battle and went back to their homes. They had no master.

184. AHAB'S SON

1 Kings 22 – 2 Kings 1

After Ahab's death, his son Ahaziah became king of Israel. He worshiped the god Baal as his parents had done. That made the Lord very angry.

Abaziah fell down through some woodwork in the palace one day and hurt himself all over.

"Go ask Baal if I am going to live," he told his messenger.

An angel of God went to Elijah and told him to find the king's messenger.

"Tell the king he will never get up from his bed again and will surely die," Elijah said.

Ahaziah became angry at Elijah. He sent fifty men out to find him, but Elijah would not go with them.

"If I am a real man of God," Elijah answered, "let fire come down and kill you all!" And a fire came down from heaven and destroyed all fifty men.

Again the king sent fifty men, and again the same thing happened. When a third group was sent, God told Elijah to go with them. Elijah went to the king and told him that God would punish him for worshiping the idol, Baal. Ahaziah died a short time later.

185. ELIJAH'S FIERY RIDE

2 Kings 2

The time had come for Elijah to turn over his job as prophet to Elisha, his helper. Elijah started to the place where he would meet God. He told Elisha to stay behind, but he followed along anyway.

Some prophets in Bethel went to Elisha to ask if he knew that his master was going away from him that day. "Yes, I know it," Elisha said, "but don't talk about it."

Elijah and Elisha went on together to the Jordan River where Elijah took off his robe. He folded it and struck the water with it. The water rolled away from them, and they were able to cross on dry land.

Elijah asked the young man what he could do for him. Elisha said he wanted a double portion of the spirit Elijah had.

Suddenly, a chariot of fire appeared from out of heaven. It parted the two men, and Elijah was taken up to heaven in a whirlwind.

Elisha saw the chariot and cried, "My father. It is the chariot of Israel!" Then Elisha cried because he would not see his great friend again.

186. MAKING WATER PURE

2 Kings 2

After Elisha watched Elijah go up to heaven, he took Elijah's robe and struck it against the water of the Jordan River. The river divided in two as it had done for Elijah. Elisha crossed over to where the other prophets had been watching.

The prophets realized that Elisha now had the powers of the prophet Elijah, but they couldn't understand what had happened to Elijah.

"Maybe the Lord has left him on top of some hill or in some valley," they said to Elisha.

Elisha told them not to go looking for Elijah because he knew that Elijah would not be coming back. But the prophets insisted.

When they returned, they followed him to Jericho. The men of that city told Elisha that their water supply was not pure. Elisha told them to bring him some salt, which he threw into the well.

"The Lord has healed these waters," he said. "The crops will grow again, and the people will be healthy."

187. WATER FOR SOLDIERS

2 Kings 3

Another of Ahab's sons named Jehoram took over the throne of Israel after his brother, Ahaziah, was killed. Jehoram was not quite as bad as the rest of his family had been in God's eyes. He put away the god Baal so the people would stop worshiping him.

Mesha, the king of Moab, had sent many thousands of lambs and sheep to King Ahab. But after the Israelite king's death, Mesha wanted his flocks back. King Jehoram asked Jehoshaphat's help in fighting the Moabite king. Together, they marched toward the battle site with their soldiers.

It took seven days to reach Edom, where the battle was to be fought. The army ran out of water on the way. King Jehoram complained that the Lord had brought them out into the desert to deliver them to the Moabite king. But Jehoshaphat was a man of God. He asked where one of God's prophets could be found who would tell them what to do.

188. DIGGING DITCHES

2 Kings 3

The kings went to visit Elisha. At first the prophet didn't want to help them because King Jehoram's parents had sought advice from their false prophets. Then he said that because Jehoshaphat followed God, he would help them.

Elisha told the soldiers to go into the valley and dig ditches. "You will not see any wind or rain," he said. "But the valley will fill up with water. Then you will win a victory over the Moabites."

By the next morning, water ran through all the ditches that the soldiers had dug. The Moabite soldiers looked across the valley at the water gleaming in the light of the red sunrise. They thought they were seeing blood. They decided the Israelites must be fighting with each other, so they marched ahead to take whatever was left of the army. When they did, the Israelites were able to defeat them.

189. A JAR OF OIL

2 Kings 4

A woman who was married to one of the prophets came to Elisha one day for help. Her husband had died and he still owed money to a man in town. The widow was afraid the man would come and take her sons away if she didn't pay him. All the widow had left was a pot of oil. Elisha told her to get all the empty pots she could find.

"Take them back to your house," he said. "Bring your sons in with you and close the door. Pour all the oil out of your pot into the empty ones."

When the widow began to pour the oil as Elisha had told her, a wonderful thing happened. One by one, she was able to fill all the spare jars with oil from her one little pot. She kept asking her sons to bring her more pots, but soon there were none left.

The woman looked down into her own jar and found that at last it was empty.

"Go and sell the oil to pay your debt," Elisha said. "There will be enough left for you and your children to live on."

190. ELISHA'S ROOM

2 Kings 4

Elisha traveled throughout the land of Israel doing God's work. He often passed through the town of Shunem where he had made friends with a rich man and woman there.

"I believe that this is a true man of God who comes by here to visit us," the woman told her husband. "We should build him a little room with a bed so he could stay overnight with us and get some rest."

Elisha asked the woman what he could do in return for her kindness. She asked for nothing.

"What can we do for this woman?" Elisha asked his servant.

Gehazi, the servant, told Elisha that the woman had no children, so Elisha promised her that by the same time the following year, she would have a son.

"Please do not lie to me," she said to Elisha.

But Elisha had told her the truth, and the baby was born the next year.

191. A TRAGEDY

2 Kings 4

The Shunammite woman cared for her little son very well. Soon he was old enough to go out with his father to the fields. He was walking among the reapers one day, helping them with their harvest, when his head began to hurt very badly.

"My head! My head!" he cried to his father.

"Carry him home to his mother," the father ordered.

The boy's mother held him and tried to comfort him all morning, but by noon he was dead. She took her little boy up to Elisha's special room and laid him on the bed. Then she called for her husband to send one of his servants to saddle up a donkey.

"I must go see the man of God," she told him.

"It's not a sabbath day," he said. "Why would you want to go see him today?"

She told him nothing about what had happened to their son and took off for Mount Carmel to look for Elisha.

192. GEHAZI AND THE STAFF

2 Kings 4

When Elisha saw the woman, he said to Gehazi, his servant, "Isn't that the Shunammite woman? Go ask her if all is well with her family."

She told Gehazi everything was fine, but when she got to the top of the mountain where Elisha stood, she fell on the ground and grabbed his ankles.

"Did I ask you for a son?" she cried. "Didn't I tell you not to lie to me about it?"

Elisha knew that something terrible must have happened to the woman's son. He told Gehzai to go back to the woman's house as fast as he could go.

"Carry my staff and lay it on the child's body," he told him.

Gehazi found the body of the Shunammite woman's son lying on the bed in Elisha's room. He took the staff and placed it on the boy as he had been told, but nothing happened. The servant walked back to tell his master that the child was dead and could not be awakened.

193. ELISHA'S MIRACLE

2 Kings 4

The boy's mother walked with Elisha back to the house. Elisha went into the boy's room alone and closed the door. He prayed to the Lord that the boy might come alive again.

Elisha lay his own body on top of the child's to bring warmth back into the lifeless body. He breathed into the boy's mouth to try and get him to breathe on his own. Soon he could feel a little heat returning to the child's body.

The prophet walked back and forth across the floor, waiting for some sign of life to appear. Then he went back and lay down on top of the child again. The child sneezed seven times and opened his eyes. The woman walked up to the room where her son had lain dead only a few minutes before.

"Take your son," Elisha said to her.

When the woman realized that her son was alive, she fell on the floor at Elisha's feet.

194. A STEW OF POISON

2 Kings 4

Elisha returned to the land of Gilgal where he met with the sons of the prophets. A famine had come to the land, and when Elisha told them to bring some food for dinner, the sons of the prophets went out to gather whatever they could find.

One of the young men found a gourd growing on a wild vine. He took it back and cut it up into pieces for the stew. Later, when they all sat down to eat, the men tasted a poison in the stew that had come from the gourd.

"This stew is poisoned!" they cried out. They stopped eating even though they were still hungry.

"Bring me some meal," Elisha said to them. He tossed some into the pot; then told them to pour what was left of the stew into their bowls. The men gobbled up every bite, and not one of them got sick.

195. HELP FROM A SLAVE

2 Kings 5

The captain of the Syrian army was a brave man named Naaman, who was well-liked by the king. Naaman had led his army in victory against the Israelites many times.

On one of his trips to battle, he captured an Israelite girl who became a servant to his wife. Naaman was the victim of a terrible skin disease called leprosy. The young Israelite girl spoke to her mistress one day about Naaman's illness.

"If only your husband could see the prophet in Samaria," she said. "He would be cured of his leprosy."

Naaman went to the king of Syria to tell him what the girl had said. The king said he would send a letter to the king of Israel to make sure that Naaman would be welcome in that country. Instead, the king of Israel took the letter as test of his power and sent Naaman away.

Elisha found out what was going on at the palace. He told the king that Naaman should come to him to be healed. A message went out to Naaman in Syria, and he left his home to go meet with the prophet of God.

196. A BATH IN THE RIVER

2 Kings 5

Naaman arrived in Israel, expecting to see Elisha. A messenger greeted the captain with instructions from the prophet.

"Go bathe in the River Jordan seven times and your skin will be like new," he said.

Naaman was not impressed by what the messenger had told him.

"The least that prophet could do is come down here and talk to me himself," Naaman said to his servants. "I expected him to call on the Lord to heal me. I don't want to go wash in that muddy old river. Our rivers in Syria are cleaner than that."

Then he started home. The soldiers who were with him spoke up: "Captain, if the prophet had asked you do something more difficult, would you have believed in him then? What difference does it make that he told you to do something simple like 'wash and be clean'?"

Naaman's soldiers had a good point. He took off his robes and went down to the River Jordan to bathe. After the seventh time, his body rose from the water and all the disease was gone from his skin.

197. GEHAZI'S SELFISH WAYS

2 Kings 5

Naaman rushed back to find Elisha and thank him for the miracle.

"I knew now that the only true God is the God of Israel," he said. "Let me give you something in return for your good works."

Elisha refused to accept any gifts from Naaman, even though the captain begged him to.

"Then let me have some of the dirt from this land to take back with me," Naaman said. "I will no longer offer sacrifice to any other god but the God of Israel."

Elisha told him to go in peace.

Elisha had done the right thing by not accepting Naaman's gifts. He knew that it was God who performed the miracle, not him. But his servant, Gehazi, had a hard time understanding why Elisha had turned down all the rich items Naaman had brought him.

"Elisha was being too generous with the Syrian," he said. "Well, if he doesn't want the gifts, I'll go run after Naaman and take some for myself."

198. TAKING GIFTS

2 Kings 5

Naaman saw Gahazi coming toward him. He thought something might be wrong, so he stopped the chariots and waited for him to catch up.

"Everything's fine," Gehazi said. "Elisha sent me to find you because he found out that two sons of the prophets are on their way from Ephraim. He wondered if he might have a few of the items you brought with you to give to them."

Naaman was delighted to give Gehazi two of everything he asked for. Gehazi hid the items away so no one would know he had them.

"Where have you been?" Elisha asked when Gehazi went in to see him.

"I haven't been anywhere," Gehazi said.

"I knew what was in your heart when you left here to follow Naaman," Elisha said. "It is not right that we should accept gifts for doing God's work. Your greed will bring you much suffering. The disease that Naaman had will be on you and your family from now on."

199. THE BLIND SOLDIERS

2 Kings 6

Peace did not last between Israel and Syria. Before long the king of Syria started raiding the Israelites in Samaria. He would tell no one but his officers about his battle plans, but the king of Israel always found out what the plans were.

The king asked his soldiers which of them was telling their secret plans. "Elisha the prophet is telling your words to the king of Israel," they said.

The next day Elisha's servants woke up to find their camp surrounded by Syrian soldiers. Elisha prayed that the soldiers would be blind to everything around them. Then he led them to the palace of the king of Israel in Samaria.

When the soldiers were inside the city of their enemy, their sight came back and they were very afraid.

"What shall I do with them?" asked the king of Israel. "Kill them?"

"No, you must feed them and send them home," Elisha said. "That is the way the Lord wants us to treat our enemies."

200. A FAMINE IN SAMARIA

2 Kings 6 - 7

Although the Syrians led no more raids against Samaria, King Ben-hadad was still determined to take the city. His army circled the city walls and prevented any food or supplies from getting to the people.

Soon the people ran out of food. They were very desperate for something to eat.

The king of Israel walked among his people and listened to their cries of hunger. He blessed Elisha and planned how to have him killed.

"The Lord has brought this evil on us," the messenger said. "Why should we wait any longer for him to do something?"

Elisha answered him, "The Lord has said that flour and barley will arrive in the town tomorrow. It will be cheap enough for everyone to afford."

"I don't see how that's possible," one of the king's men said.

"You will see it," Elisha said. "But you won't get any of it because you doubted the Lord's word."

201. THE LEPERS

2 Kings 7

Four men who had leprosy were sitting outside the gate of Samaria. They couldn't go inside because of their disease, and they were very hungry.

"We would die of hunger even if we could get in the city," they said. "The Syrians have all the food. Let's surrender to them and see if they will give us something to eat."

While the four lepers were on their way to the enemy camp, God sent the sound of rumbling chariots and horses' hooves into the Syrian camp. The soldiers thought they were being attacked, so they ran away and left everything behind.

When the lepers finally reached the camp they were surprised to see that no one was there. They sat down to enjoy the food and ate until they could eat no more. Then they picked up gold and silver treasures and hid them in their clothes.

202. FOOD FOR THE PEOPLE

2 Kings 7

After a while, the lepers began to think about what they were doing.

"We have found all this good fortune, yet we haven't told our people about it," they said. "We'd better let them know what we have found before we get in trouble."

The lepers carried the news of the deserted enemy camp back to the palace guards. The guards woke the king up from his sleep to tell him the news.

"This is just a trick," he said. "Those Syrians are hiding out there somewhere, waiting for us to show up."

The king agreed to send a few soldiers to check out the lepers' story. When they came back unharmed, the people ran to the camp as fast as they could to get something to eat.

The mob of people was so wild that they trampled the king's messenger who was standing by the gate. Even though he had seen the food, he died before he could eat any of it, just as Elisha, the prophet, had said.

203. A PROPHECY OF EVIL

2 Kings 8

Ben-hadad, the king of Syria, became very sick. He heard through his servants that Elisha the prophet was in the Syrian city of Damascus for a visit. The king sent for his trusted servant, Hazael, and told him to ask Elisha if he would recover from his illness.

Elisha told Hazael to tell Ben-hadad that he would get better. But Elisha knew that was not true. He began to cry and Hazael asked him what was wrong.

"The Lord has already told me that you will be the next king of Syria," Elisha said. "You will do many terrible things to the people of Israel."

Hazel told him that was a foolish prophecy. He went back to the palace and told the king that he would be better soon.

The next day, Hazael took a thick cloth and wet it with water. He went to Ben-hadad's room and held it over his face until he died. Then he took over Ben-hadad's throne and became the king of Syria.

204. KING JEHU

2 Kings 9

Elisha sent a young prophet to find Jehu, the son of Jehoshaphat. "Take some of this oil to anoint his head and tell him he is to be the next king of Israel," the prophet said. "After you've done that, run back here as fast as you can."

The young man found Jehu sitting with some other army captains. He asked if he could talk to Jehu in private. When he had poured the oil over Jehu's head as Elisha had told him, he spoke to the captain.

"The Lord has said that you are to be the next king of Israel. You will destroy the house of Ahab because Jezebel caused all of God's prophets to be killed. Jezebel's body will be left in the streets and no one will bury her."

The young man ran away, and Jehu went back to where the

other captains were sitting. When he told them what happened, the men jumped up and took off their robes to place on the stairs under Jehu's feet. They blew their trumpets and shouted, "Jehu is king!"

205. A WILD RIDER

2 Kings 9

King Joram of Israel had come to Jezreel to rest after he was injured in a battle with King Hazael of Syria. Jehu began to plot how he could take Joram's place as king.

Guards at the palace saw Jehu and his soldiers riding toward Jezreel and went to tell the king. Joram sent a messenger to see if the riders came in peace, but Jehu persuaded the messenger to join his troops. Finally Joram went out to meet the mysterious rider.

"Do you come in peace, Jehu?" Joram asked.

"What kind of peace can exist as long as your evil mother, Jezebel, still worships her false gods?"

Joram turned to King Ahaziah of Judah who was with him and said, "This is treason!" They tried to get away, but Jehu killed them both.

206. JEZEBEL DIES

2 Kings 9

Jehu entered the gates of Jezreel. Jezebel heard that he was on his way, so she fixed her hair and makeup and went to her window to watch for him.

"Do you think you will have any peace now that you have murdered the king?" she yelled at Jehu.

"Who up there is on my side?" he yelled back.

Three men showed their faces at the window.

"Throw her down!" Jehu said.

The men picked Jezebel up and threw her out the window. The horses ran over her dead body in the street.

Even though Jehu went back later to find her body, there was nothing left. The prophecy of Elijah had come true. The wicked queen's body would never be buried.

207. A SECRET KING

2 Kings 11

After Jehu killed Ahaziah, his mother, Athaliah, became queen of Judah. Like her mother, Jezebel, Athaliah was a mean and violent woman. She had all the rest of the royal family killed so that none of them could take her place on the throne. One of the family members was able to hide Ahaziah's son with a priest named Jehoiada. He stayed there for six years while Athaliah was queen.

The little boy, Joash, was only seven years old when Jehoiada decided it was time for the true prince to take the throne from the evil Athaliah. Jehoiada asked the palace guards and captains to come to the temple. After he had made them promise not to tell anyone what they were about to see, he brought Joash into the room and told them who he was.

All the guards agreed to stay on duty to guard the prince. They formed a circle and kept their weapons ready. Then Jehoiada brought the boy out and put a crown on the boy's head. The boy Joash was king.

208. THE KING AND THE PRIEST

2 Chronicles 23 - 24

After Joash was crowned, the people ran into the streets, cheering for their new king. Athaliah followed the people to the temple where young Joash stood surrounded by trumpeters and members of the court.

"Treason! Treason!" she cried.

Jehoiada sent soldiers in to capture the former queen. He told them to take her away and kill her outside the temple area.

The priest had the new king and all his people promise to follow God from then on. Then they went to the house of Baal to break down the altars and do away with all the idols. The Levites were brought back to lead the services of the temple. Jehoiada saw to it that everything was done according to God's laws.

Because Joash was such a young boy when he became king, Jehoiada stayed at his side to guide him. The priest helped the king seek God's advice in many matters.

209. FIXING THE TEMPLE

2 Chronicles 24

Joash grew up to be a good ruler. He wanted to do what was best for his people. For many years the temple where the people worshiped had not been cared for. The kings and queens who worshiped idols had paid no attention to God's house. To repair all the damage would take a lot of money.

The king ordered a chest to be placed at the entrance to the temple to put money in. The collection was taken from the people every week, so it wasn't long before there was enough money to begin the repairs.

Many workers were brought in to do the job. Carpenters, stone masons, and metal workers rebuilt the temple to look as fine as it had when Solomon first built it.

Joash and Jehoiada were very pleased when the temple was finished. The people of Judah went there to pray and offer sacrifice to God, and everything went well in their country for many years.

210. A CHANGE OF HEART

2 Chronicles 24

Together, King Joash and Jehoiada the priest made a powerful team. But after Jehoiada died, the king was not so strong. Some of the princes wanted Joash to bring back idol worship. They put pressure on him until he finally gave in.

Jehoiada's son, Zechariah, was a man of God as his father had been. He tried to make the people turn away from the idols. King Joash ordered the people to stone Zechariah to death for going against him.

"The Lord has seen what you have done, and he will punish you for it," Zechariah told Joash. But Joash didn't want to hear that and he had Zechariah stoned in the courtyard.

At the end of that year, a Syrian army marched against the country of Judah. Joash's army was not strong enough, and the Syrians defeated the Israelites.

King Joash was wounded badly in the battle. While he lay in his bed, some of his soldiers came to his room and killed him to get revenge for Zechariah's death.

211. SOLDIERS FOR HIRE

2 Chronicles 25

Amaziah, Joash's son, became king of Judah, and he followed God's laws. Most of Amaziah's energy was spent building a great army to go out and conquer other lands. He called upon 300,000 Israelite soldiers to fight against the Edomites.

But Amaziah didn't think that would be enough, so he hired 100,000 more soldiers from another Israelite tribe. God did not want him to do that.

A prophet from God came to ask King Amaziah to change his mind.

"What about all the silver and gold I've already paid these men?" Amaziah said. "I'll never get it back."

"The Lord will repay you much more than that," said the prophet.

Amaziah decided to let the soldiers go. He led the soldiers of Judah into battle against the Edomites, and God helped him to defeat them.

212. A BIG DEFEAT

2 Chronicles 25

A maziah should have been very grateful to God for his help in the battle. But he found out that the hired soldiers had come back to Samaria while he was away. Amaziah turned away from God and allowed the Edomite prisoners to set up their idols and worship them. Soon the people of Judah started to worship them, too.

God sent a prophet to Amaziah to try to get him to change his mind about the idols. The king was annoyed with the prophet and would not listen. He sent the prophet away and ordered a messenger to tell the king of Israel to prepare to fight.

The Israelite king became tired of Amaziah's boasting. "Come out and let's see how tough you really are," he said.

Israel not only won the battle against Judah; they chased Amaziah back to Jerusalem and destroyed much of that city, too. The people were very upset at their king for starting a war he couldn't win. Amaziah ran away but they found him and killed him.

213. THE PRIESTS' WARNING

2 Chronicles 25

A maziah's son Uzziah repaired much of the damage done to the country of Judah. He built towers around the city of Jerusalem and made it safer from attack.

Uzziah wanted to lead the people in the ways of God. He listened to God's prophets and did as they told him. God rewarded him with riches and power.

One day Uzziah had become so powerful that he thought he could do anything he wanted. There was a place in the temple called the sanctuary where only the high priests were allowed to go. Uzziah went in and began to burn some incense in a bowl.

"You're not supposed to be in here," the priests said to him. "Leave now before you dishonor the Lord."

Uzziah didn't listen to the priests' warning. As he stood there, lighting the incense, leprosy began to spread over his skin. Uzziah was a victim of the disease from then on, and was sent to a place away from the palace to live out his life with other lepers.

214. ELISHA DIES

2 Kings 13

The people of Judah and Israel were ruled by many different kings over the years. Following the death of King Solomon, the tribes remained divided. God had told Jehu that four generations of his family would reign in Israel. Jehu's grandson was Israel's leader when the prophet Elisha became sick and knew he would soon die.

The king rushed to Elisha's side and wept because the Syrians were about to attack again.

"Take that bow and arrow," Elisha said to him. "Open the window and shoot the arrow eastward."

Elisha put his hands over the king's hands and they shot the arrow. Elisha said that represented the Lord's deliverance of his people from the Syrians.

"Now take the arrows and strike the floor," Elisha said.

The king hit the floor with them three times.

"You should have hit the floor five or six times," said Elisha, "so you would be able to destroy Syria completely. Now you will be able to beat them only three times."

215. SUMMER FRUIT

2 Kings 14 – 15, Amos

After Elisha died, there was no prophet to take his place. The new king of Israel, Jeroboam II, did as he pleased because there was no man of God around to guide him.

A shepherd named Amos came from his home in Judah one day to sell wool in Israel. When he entered the marketplace in Bethel, no one knew that God had sent him as a prophet to warn them.

Amos told the traders that they must stop cheating the poor people who came to buy from them. He criticized the rich people for keeping all their wealth to themselves. He warned them that they were so unjust that God would send a great punishment to them all.

"God showed me a basket of late summer fruit," Amos told them. "He said the season of my people is at an end. I will not pass by them anymore."

The people did not like what Amos said, and they sent him back to his home in Judah.

216. AN UNFAITHFUL LAND

Hosea

God chose a man named Hosea to deliver a message about his love for his people. He told Hosea to take a wife from among the women who were not pure.

Hosea obeyed God and married a woman named Gomer. They had a son and a daughter, but Gomer soon left Hosea. God came to tell him what he should do next.

"My relationship with the people of Israel is much the same as yours is with your wife, Gomer," God said. "You gave her a home and children, and now she has left you just like my people have turned away from me."

God knew that Hosea still loved Gomer. "You must go and bring her back," God said. "The people of Israel have been unfaithful to me many times, but I have always taken them back."

Hosea found his wife and brought her home. Then he told the people of Israel that they must come back to God, too.

"The Lord will forgive you," he said.

217. AN UNWILLING PROPHET

Jonah 1

God called upon some people who were not as willing to be prophets as Amos and Hosea. One time God called a man named Jonah to go to the city of Nineveh in the country of Assyria.

"You must warn the people of Nineveh that if they don't change their wicked ways, I will punish them," God said.

Jonah didn't want to go to Nineveh because the Assyrians were mean people who treated outsiders very badly. He decided to take off for a place called Joppa, where he boarded a ship. Thinking he was safe, Jonah went below the deck of the boat and fell sound asleep. The captain awakened Jonah a while later.

"Why are you asleep?" the captain yelled. "There is a great storm upon us. Call on your God to save us!"

Jonah came back on deck to find that a mighty wind was sending waves over the bow of the boat.

"What has caused this evil to come upon us?" the captain asked. "We must see which one of us is to blame for this."

218. MAN OVERBOARD

Jonah 1

The passengers and crew wrote their names down and threw them all together. Jonah was not surprised that his name was drawn out.

"What will we do with you to make this storm go away?" the people asked.

Jonah knew that as long as he was on board, the storm would continue, and they might all be drowned.

"Throw me overboard," he said.

The men on the ship didn't want to go that far. They knew Jonah would die for sure if they did. So they rowed as hard as they could to try to reach the shore.

"Please, Lord," they prayed, "don't let us die because of what this man has done."

But the storm got worse, and the sailors had no other choice but to throw Jonah into the sea. After they had done it, the water calmed down and the clouds broke up overhead. The men offered a sacrifice to God and made a promise to follow the Lord for the rest of their lives.

219. THE GIANT FISH

Jonah 1 - 4

God saved the men on the boat and he also had a plan to save Jonah. He sent a giant fish to swallow Jonah. The fish didn't eat him, though, and Jonah stayed in its belly for three days.

Jonah prayed to God in the darkness. He thanked the Lord for saving him and promised to do whatever God asked of him from then on.

God made the great fish swim close to the land and spit up Jonah on the shore. Then God asked Jonah again to go to the city of Nineveh. This time Jonah obeyed God as he had promised. He told the people that their city would be destroyed in forty days if they did not turn away from their evil deeds.

The people believed what God said. The king ordered them not to eat or drink for several days to show their obedience to God. When God saw that the people wanted to be forgiven, their city was saved.

220. ASSYRIANS TAKE OVER

2 Kings 17

Even though God had given the Assyrians in Nineveh the opportunity to follow him, they were soon back to their evil ways. The people of Israel, too, had turned from God despite all the prophets' warnings.

Hoshea was the leader of Israel when the Assyrians attacked again. The Assyrian king made Hoshea pay him taxes so the Assyrians would not attack Israel.

The king of Israel decided he had had enough of this sort of blackmail, so he sent to the king of Egypt for advice. That year Hoshea did not send any tax money to King Shalmaneser in Assyria. The king did not like being double-crossed. He sent his army to Samaria to attack the Israelites.

After three years of fighting, the Israel soldiers could no longer battle the Assyrians. The Assyrian forces marched in and captured the Israelites. It was a sad day for the people who had refused to listen to the prophets of the land.

221. FOREIGNERS INVADE

2 Kings 17

The Assyrians were cruel and powerful, and they took the Israelites out of their land to live in Assyria.

Samaria became a land of foreigners. The Assyrian king sent people from many places to live in the Israelite city. They brought with them many kinds of idols. Each group had their own god, and none of them followed in the ways of the one true God.

Ahaz, the king of Judah, had heard about what had happened to the Israelites at the hands of the Assyrians. He knew what the soldiers were capable of, but since Ahaz was an idol-worshiper, he did not ask God for help.

The foreigners who had taken over Israel sided with Syria, another powerful nation, and against Assyria. Then they attacked Judah, hoping to force King Ahaz to join their cause and fight with them against the Assyrians.

222. AHAZ PAYS A PRICE

2 Kings 16, Isaiah 7

King Ahaz didn't know what to do. A prophet named Isaiah was living in Judah at the time, and God sent him to the king with a message.

"You must not be so fearful of these two armies," Isaiah said to the king. "God has said that the leaders of these armies will not be able to accomplish what they have come to do.

"If you will believe what the Lord has said, no harm will come to you," Isaiah continued. "But if you don't, your kingdom will fall."

Ahaz did not believe that God would help him. He felt that he had to take matters into his own hands to get rid of the Syrian and Israelite armies. He sent a messenger to the king of Assyria to ask for his protection.

The Assyrians were all too happy to help—for a price. Ahaz took gold and silver from the temple as well as the treasures from his own house to pay the Assyrians. He also promised to be loyal to them for the rest of his reign. The Assyrians had succeeded in taking complete control of Judah.

223. SAVED FROM THE ENEMY

2 Kings 18 - 19

When King Ahaz died, he left behind his debt to the Assyrians for his son, Hezekiah. The Assyrians found out that Hezekiah had broken down the altars to the idols, and they planned to attack Judah.

Hezekiah tried to pay off the Assyrians as his father had done, but it didn't work. The Assyrian king sent troops to the city walls of Jerusalem to force the people to surrender without a fight.

"Your God can't save you," they yelled. "The king of Assyria is your only hope."

But the people would not answer the soldiers. The Assyrian king sent word to King Hezekiah that the people of Judah had better surrender. Hezekiah went to the temple to pray and sent messengers to ask the prophet Isaiah for advice. Isaiah told him that God would protect the city of Jerusalem from its enemies.

That night the angel of death visited the Assyrian camp. The next morning thousands of Assyrian soldiers lay dead. The king took what was left of his army and went away from the gates of Jerusalem. Isaiah's words had come true.

224. THE SIGN OF THE SHADOW

2 Kings 20

King Hezekiah got very sick, and Isaiah came to tell him that he would not live much longer.

Hezekiah began to cry and pray. "Remember how I have done the things that were good for you, O Lord."

God heard Hezekiah's prayers. He stopped Isaiah as he was leaving the palace.

"Go back and tell Hezekiah that I have seen his tears and I will heal him in three days," God said. "Also tell him that I will add fifteen years to his life."

When Isaiah delivered God's message, Hezekiah asked what sign God would give to let him know he would get better. Isaiah told him that the shadow on the sundial they used as a clock would go backward, not forward.

Isaiah prayed for the sign to appear, and the shadow on the dial moved back ten degrees. King Hezekiah knew God would heal him.

225. GOD'S LAWS ARE FOUND

2 Kings 21 - 22

King Hezekiah lived for fifteen more years as a gift from God. His son Manasseh took over the throne of Judah. He brought the people back to idol worship worse than ever. He even constructed altars to the false gods in the temple!

Fortunately, Manasseh's grandson Josiah soon replaced his wicked grandfather as king of Judah. Josiah loved God. He wanted to repair all the damage Manasseh had done to God's temple.

A lot of money was collected from the people of Judah to begin the work. Josiah told his scribe Shaphan to have the High Priest Hilkiah distribute the money among the workers for their materials.

Shortly after work began, Hilkiah found a scroll buried in the temple. Shaphan took the scroll to King Josiah and read it to him.

"These are the laws that God gave to his people," he said. "We are in a lot of trouble because no one has followed many of these rules for years."

226. A TIME OF PEACE

2 Kings 22 - 23

Josiah sent Shaphan to find a prophet who could tell them what would happen next. A prophetess named Huldah was living in Jerusalem. God had given her a message for Josiah and the people of Judah.

"I will bring evil to everyone in Judah because they turned away from me so many times," God said. "But tell the king of Judah who sent for you that he will not see the destruction of the land in his lifetime. He has been a good servant, and I promise that he will live and die in peace."

After Josiah heard God's message, he tried to convince his people that it was more important than ever to follow God's laws. He read the scrolls to them and made a new promise to obey God's commandments.

Next Josiah and his men went about the land destroying every idol they could find. They killed the priests who worshiped the false gods and ran off all the magicians and wizards.

The people were very happy with their king, and they followed Josiah until the day he died.

227. BEGINNING OF THE END

Jeremiah 1

God had kept the people of Judah safe as he had promised. Even after Josiah died, he was willing to forgive his people if they would love and serve him.

A young man named Jeremiah was studying to be a priest like his father. Long before he was born, God had chosen him to be a prophet. Jeremiah could not believe that God wanted him to take on such a great task.

"I cannot speak well," Jeremiah said. "Besides, I'm only a child."

God touched his mouth and said, "Look now! I have put the words in your mouth. You will spread my words throughout the nations."

God told Jeremiah to look at a pot that was boiling over.

"I will send an enemy from the north to surround Judah. The evil will spill over like the pot," God told Jeremiah. "You must go tell the people what will become of them if they keep on worshiping their false gods."

228. THE OXEN'S YOKE

Jeremiah 27

While Judah and Israel were going from one evil king to another, the nearby country of Babylon was ruled by a powerful king named Nebuchadnezzar.

Jeremiah came to talk to King Zedekiah one day about God's plans for the country, but Zedekiah did not want to listen to him. Zedekiah thought he could find some other countries to help him fight Babylon.

God told Jeremiah that he must do something to show the people they were wrong about the Babylonians. Jeremiah took a wooden yoke that was used to harness the oxen for ploughing. He lifted it up and put it over his own neck and walked out into the crowd.

"If you will serve under the yoke of the king of Babylon, the Lord will let you live peacefully in your own land," Jeremiah told them.

229. THROWN IN A WELL

Jeremiah 37 - 38

Jeremiah continued to spread God's message, but the leaders of the country got very tired of listening to him. His message sounded cowardly to them. They went to King Zedekiah to see if something could be done about him.

First the leaders put Jeremiah in a prison cell. But Jeremiah continued to shout his messages from God to the people who gathered around the prison.

Then they marched Jeremiah to an old well that no longer had any water in it. They lowered him into the dark, muddy pit and left him there to die.

A member of the court whose name was Ebed-Melech heard what the leaders had done to the prophet, and ran to the king to tell him.

The king sent Ebed-Melech and some other men to rescue Jeremiah. They brought the prophet back to the palace. This time King Zedekiah was ready to listen to what Jeremiah had to say, but it was too late.

230. JERUSALEM DESTROYED

2 Kings 25

When King Nebuchadnezzar arrived outside the city of Jerusalem, King Zedekiah refused to surrender as Jeremiah had told him to.

The Babylonian soldiers set up camp outside the city gates and refused to let any food come inside to the people. Soon they were starving.

King Zedekiah knew he had made a mistake in holding out against the Babylonians. He tried to run away, but the Babylonian soldiers captured him. Then they attacked the city and burned down all the important buildings, including the temple.

The Babylonians took most of the people captive as well. Only the poorest people were allowed to stay to work in the vineyards and fields.

Jeremiah stayed behind in Judah with them. He knew the people needed to hear God's word.

231. PROPHET IN BABYLON

Ezekiel 1 – 5

While Jeremiah remained in Jerusalem, another prophet spoke to God's people who were prisoners in Babylon. Ezekiel was a young man who had studied to be a priest in God's temple. One day God sent a special vision to Ezekiel.

"I want you to deliver my word to the people of Israel," God said. "Do not be rebellious like them; do as I say so you can help them."

Instead of sending Ezekiel to talk with the people, God told him to act out his messages so that the people could see the truth.

Ezekiel drew a map of Jerusalem on a clay tablet. Then he took an iron pan to represent the gates of the city. He lay his head against it to show that an enemy would camp at the gates of Jerusalem. He put out a small portion of food on the ground so the people would see that they would soon run out of food.

Ezekiel acted out many scenes to show the people how much they had disobeyed God.

232. LIVING BONES

Ezekiel 37

Many of Ezekiel's messages were warnings to the people. But God still wanted them to have hope for the future. He led Ezekiel out to a field one day to show him what would become of Judah and Israel. The field was full of old, dried-up bones.

"Can these bones come to life again?" God asked his prophet.

"Lord, you are the one who knows that," Ezekiel answered.

So the Lord commanded Ezekiel to speak to the bones and tell them to listen to God's words. He promised that God would breathe life into them again. While he was speaking, Ezekiel heard a rattling noise. The bones started to come back together and form human bodies.

"These bones represent the people of Israel," God said to Ezekiel. "Look how they are coming back to life. One day my people will come back to live in their own land. Then they will know the power of their God."

233. DANIEL IN BABYLON

Daniel 1

When King Nebuchadnezzar had attacked Jerusalem the first time, he told his adviser to pick out several of the most handsome and smartest young Israelite prisoners. He wanted to educate these boys in the ways of the Babylonians.

The adviser picked a boy named Daniel. He also brought along three of his friends whom he called Shadrach, Meshach, and Abednego. The boys were taken to a separate place to live and study.

"You will eat the same food and wine that is served to the king every day," the adviser said to them.

Daniel did not think that was such a good idea. He and his friends had been raised by the laws of God. They knew that eating the same food the king of Babylon ate would be wrong.

Daniel and his friends were determined to follow in the ways of God even though they were living in a foreign land. God rewarded them by giving them great wisdom.

234. THE KING'S DREAM

Daniel 2

King Nebuchadnezzar had a dream one night that upset him. He called to all the magicians and astrologers in his court to ask them what the dream meant.

"Tell us your dream," they said.

"That's the problem," the king said. "I don't remember it exactly. You must tell me what it was about. If you can't do that, I'll have you all killed."

The magicians begged the king not to kill them.

"There is no one alive who can tell what another person has dreamed," they said.

That just made the king more angry. He commanded all the wise men in the kingdom to be killed. Daniel heard what the king was planning.

"I will tell the king what he wants to know," Daniel said.

Daniel hurried to find Meshach, Shadrach, and Abednego. He told them all to pray for God's answer to the meaning of the king's dream.

That night King Nebuchadnezzar's dream came to Daniel in a vision. He woke up praising the Lord for giving him such great wisdom.

235. A DREAM REVEALED

Daniel 2

Daniel went before the king the next morning to tell him the meaning of his dream.

"None of the magicians or wizards you asked could tell you

what your dream meant," he said. "Your dream was a message from God."

"You saw a great image of a man made of many metals," Daniel said. "The head was of gold, the chest of silver, the thighs of brass, the legs of iron, and the feet were made of clay. While you were watching the image, a mighty rock broke away from the hillside and rolled down upon the image. It broke the clay feet off the image and caused it to fall."

Daniel told the king that the image represented the kingdom of Nebuchadnezzar. He was the golden head of the image because he was the most powerful king who would ever sit on the throne of Babylon.

"One day God will send his own powerful kingdom to destroy the others," Daniel said. "That kingdom will be like the rock you saw in your dream."

236. THE GOLDEN IMAGE

Daniel 3

King Nebuchadnezzar could not get the picture of the golden image he dreamed about out of his mind. Daniel had told him that the golden head represented his power, so he decided to build a statue of his own image so everyone would see him as their great king.

When the statue was finished, it stood tall above the men of the city. The king sent out a message that all the people were to come to the statue and bow before it when he gave the signal. All the people obeyed except for Shadrach, Meshach, and Abednego. They knew it was against God's commandment to bow down before an idol.

The king had told his servants to watch for anyone who did not do as the king asked. They were to be brought before the king and thrown in a huge furnace as punishment. One of the servants reported that Daniel's friends had not obeyed the king.

237. INTO THE FURNACE

Daniel 3

The three men stood calmly before King Nebuchadnezzar as they listened to his angry threats.

"If you agree to go out and bow before my statue, I will give you another chance to save your lives," the king told them. "If not, I'll have to throw you in the furnace. Will your God be able to save you from that?"

"We cannot speak for our Lord," the three answered. "We only know that if he wants to, God can deliver us safely out of the furnace. No matter what God chooses, we will not bow down to your golden idol."

The king was enraged at the three men's disobedience. He decided he would really show them a lesson.

"Make the fire hotter," he commanded.

The servants who were tending the furnace made the fire so hot that they were burned when they threw Shadrach, Meshach, and Abednego into the flames.

238. A FOURTH MAN APPEARS

Daniel 2

Nebuchadnezzar watched as the flames rose up. Suddenly, he jumped out of his seat and ran to where his advisers were standing.

"Didn't we just put three men into that furnace?" he said. "I now see four men walking in the flames. One of them looks like an angel of God."

The king yelled into the furnace. "Shadrach, Meshach, and Abednego, you servants of God. Come out!"

The king's advisers gathered around the three men as they walked out of the furnace. They were amazed! The men had not been harmed at all by the flames.

"Bless the god of Shadrach, Meshach, and Abednego," the king said. "He has sent an angel to save his servants from death."

King Nebuchadnezzar sent a message to the people of Babylon, telling them that no one must ever say anything against God or they would be punished. He then rewarded Shadrach, Meshach, and Abednego by giving them all promotions within the government of Babylon.

239. A TALL TREE

Daniel 4

King Nebuchadnezzar was very proud of his great kingdom. He boasted a lot about all he had done, but he forgot to be thankful to the Lord who had given him all these things.

God sent another message to the king in a dream one night. The next morning Nebuchadnezzar called in all his wise men to tell him what his strange dream had meant. Daniel came before the king and listened as the king spoke.

"I saw a tall, beautiful tree that had a strong trunk. It was full of leaves and fruit. All the animals came to stand underneath it for shelter," the king said.

"But then I heard a voice that sounded like an angel's. It commanded that the tree be cut down. Only the stump was left. The stump was like a man, and the angel said that the heart of the man would be changed into a beast. What does all this mean?" he asked Daniel.

240. THE KING'S LESSON

Daniel 4

Daniel seemed upset by what he had heard. The king told him that no matter how bad the news was, he wanted to hear it.

"That tree in your dream is really you," Daniel said. "You have a great kingdom that feeds and provides shelter for many people. You have taken all the credit for this kingdom for yourself. You have left God out, and now he will strike you down like the tree and send you out in the desert to live like a beast for seven years."

At first the king was frightened by what Daniel had said. But nearly a year went by and nothing happened, so he went back to his boastful and proud ways.

One day he was walking around the palace, bragging about what a great kingdom he had built, when he suddenly had a fit of madness. He turned into a beast-like creature and remained that way for seven years until he remembered to honor God as the one and only true king.

241. WRITING ON THE WALL

Daniel 5

After the reign of King Nebuchadnezzar, King Belshazzar came to the throne of Babylon.

One night Belshazzar threw a big party for a thousand of his officials and captains. He ordered his servants to bring out the golden cups that King Nebuchadnezzar had stolen from the temple in Jerusalem. They poured them full of wine and drank from them.

Suddenly, the king looked up to see a hand writing a message on the wall. He yelled for someone to come quickly and tell him what the message meant.

Daniel told the king that the message was from God. By bringing out the sacred cups from the temple to use at his party, the king had displeased God.

"The writing on the wall means that your reign as king will soon be over," Daniel said.

That night an army from an enemy country crept into Babylon and killed the king.

242. JEALOUSY IN THE LAND

Daniel 6

Before King Belshazzar was killed, he had made Daniel a high-ranking official in the government. King Darius, who took over the throne of Babylon when the Medes and Persians conquered the land, realized how wise Daniel was. He let him stay as a ruler of one of the Babylonian regions.

There were men in other regions who held the same important job as Daniel. They were very jealous of Daniel because they thought the king treated him better. They wanted to catch Daniel breaking some law so they could get rid of him.

They got the king to sign a law making it illegal for anyone to pray for anything from any leader or god except the king. Anyone who broke the law would be lowered into a pit of hungry lions.

Daniel knew about the new law, but that did not stop him from praying to God every day as he had done all his life. The men waited and watched Daniel's house so they could catch him in the act.

243. THE LIONS' DEN

Daniel 6

Some of the men watched as Daniel kneeled down to pray to God. He prayed three times each day on his knees in front of the window. They ran back to tell the king that they had found someone breaking his new law. When King Darius found out who the guilty person was, he was very sad. He knew Daniel was a good man.

"Your god will deliver you from the lions," King Darius said as Daniel was lowered into the pit.

The king could not sleep at all that night. As soon as dawn came, he ran to the lion pit and ordered the guards to remove the stone.

"Daniel!" he yelled into the dark hole. "Did the god whom you serve so faithfully keep you safe from the lions?"

Daniel answered him in a hurry. "My God sent his angel to shut the lions' mouths so they couldn't harm me. He knows I am innocent and have done nothing wrong before the king."

The king commanded that Daniel be released from the lions' den immediately. He sent for the evil men who had made him sign the unjust law and threw them in with the lions.

244. VISIONS OF THE FUTURE

Daniel 9, 12

In all the days that Daniel spent in Babylon, his one wish was that someday his people could go back to Jerusalem and reclaim their city.

One day he was reading the book of the prophet Jeremiah. It said that seventy years would go by before the people of Israel could return to their homeland. Daniel began to pray to the Lord for that time to come.

While Daniel was praying, the Angel Gabriel came down from heaven to speak with him. He told Daniel that God had heard his prayers and that the people of Israel would be going home soon.

"You must go back to Jerusalem to rebuild the city," the angel said. "Then God will send a savior to remove all your sins."

Gabriel told Daniel many things about what life would be like in the time of the savior's coming. Daniel understood most of these things, but some he did not. However, Daniel went on living his life and trusting the Lord each day.

245. HOME TO JERUSALEM

Ezra 1 - 3

King Cyrus was the next king to rule Babylon. The seventy years of captivity prophesied by Jeremiah had come true, so God filled the king's heart, and Cyrus went out to talk to the people.

"The Lord has been very good to me," he said. "Now he has asked that I send his people back to rebuild the temple in Jerusalem. You are free to go back to your homeland!"

Everyone was thrilled with the king's news. Even the people who decided to stay behind were happy that the temple would be built again.

Once they were back in Jerusalem, the people set to work. Almost everything had been destroyed, so there was much to do. The priests Jeshua and Zerubbabel helped collect the money and materials to get started on the temple.

Nearly two years passed before the work was actually begun. When the foundation was laid for the new temple, everyone came out to celebrate and to praise the Lord for sending them back home.

246. TROUBLE AT THE TEMPLE

Ezra 4 - 6

Many of the Israelites' enemies still lived in the land that surrounded Jerusalem. When they heard that the people were returning to rebuild the temple, they wanted to do something to stop them.

One group called the Samaritans sent people to the temple to bother the workers. They sent letters complaining about the Israelites to every king and ruler they could think of. In one letter to the king of Persia, they said that if the Israelites were allowed to live in Jerusalem again, they would not pay their taxes.

Two Israelite government officials decided to send a letter to the king of Babylon, telling the story of how King Cyrus had sent the Israelites back to Jerusalem to rebuild the temple.

"King Cyrus wrote a decree," the letter said. "If you will look where his things are kept, you will find it."

Once the decree was located, the king of Babylon wrote one himself, ordering everyone to leave the Israelites alone and let them rebuild their temple.

247. THE WALLS OF JERUSALEM

Nehemiah 1 - 4

Nehemiah had stayed behind in Babylon when his people had returned to Jerusalem. He had a very important job as a wine steward for King Artaxerxes.

One evening the king noticed that his wine steward looked very upset. He asked Nehemiah what was the matter.

"I am sad for my people in Jerusalem," Nehemiah said. "If it is all right with you, I would like very much to go back and help them out."

Nehemiah assembled a group of workers to start rebuilding the wall around the city of Jerusalem. Often, while they were working, some of their enemies would come up and yell mean things at them. One time the Samaritans even threatened to attack the workers. Nehemiah told his men to keep their weapons with them while they worked.

A guard was posted to warn the Israelites if any enemies approached. They went on with their work until a great wall had been built around the city of Jerusalem for protection.

248. THE KINGDOM OF PERSIA

Esther 1

After the wall was built around Jerusalem, the people inside the city felt much safer than they had for some time. The Israelites who had stayed behind in Babylon were not so lucky. Persian soldiers had taken over the country of Babylonia and made it a part of the Persian Empire.

King Ahasuerus was a powerful and selfish ruler. During a party he was giving one night, he told his queen, Vashti, to come meet his friends. The men were all very drunk, and Vashti refused to be around them. Ahasuerus was very angry. His advisors talked him into getting rid of Vashti so that the other men's wives would not think that they could refuse their husbands too.

Not long after that, the king became lonely for his queen. He sent for all the young women in the country to come before him so he could pick a new queen.

249. QUEEN ESTHER

Esther 2 - 3

An Israelite named Mordecai was working in the palace for the king. Mordecai's beautiful young cousin named Esther lived with him. He had taken care of the girl since her parents had died. When Mordecai heard about the king's request, he told Esther not to tell the king that she was a Jew.

The king chose Esther from among all the other girls because she was clearly the most beautiful one of all. He made her his queen and held a great feast to celebrate.

Around that same time, Mordecai heard of a plot by two men to kill the king. He told Esther about it, and she was able to warn the king before any harm could come to him.

King Ahasuerus appointed a man named Haman to be the head of his government. Haman commanded everyone in the palace to bow down to him, and everyone obeyed the command—except Queen Esther's cousin, Mordecai!

250. AN EVIL PLAN

Esther 3

Haman couldn't understand why Mordecai refused to do as he asked, so he sent some of his men to find out more about Mordecai. The servants soon reported that Mordecai was a Jew. He would not bow before anyone but God.

This news made Haman very angry. He set out to find a way to get rid of all the Jews living in Persia. He went to the king with a plan.

"These people called the Jews are scattered all over the kingdom," Haman said. "They follow their own laws instead of yours. If you sign a law permitting them to be killed, I will put a lot of silver in your treasury."

Once the king had agreed, Haman wrote a law that allowed the Jews in the kingdom to be killed on a certain day. And any of their possessions could be taken.

The law was posted throughout the land. It was a time of great sorrow for the Jews.

251. ESTHER'S PLAN

Esther 4 – 5

When Mordecai heard about the law, he cried in sorrow. He sent word to Esther asking for her help.

"You must go before the king to speak for your people," he told her. But she replied that she could not because the king would kill anyone who came before him without being asked.

"Don't you know you will die anyway if this law is allowed to stand?" Mordecai pleaded with her. So the queen told him to gather all the Jews together to pray for her before she went in to see the king.

Esther was very frightened when she entered the king's room, but the king held out the golden scepter to her to show that she was welcome in his sight.

"What has brought you here, Esther?" he asked. "What is your request?"

Esther told him that she wanted to invite him and Haman to dinner that evening. The king gladly accepted and called for Haman to come as well.

252. THE GALLOWS

Esther 5

That night as they were seated at the dinner table, the king asked Esther again what she would like him to do for her.

"I only ask that you and Haman join me again tomorrow night for a banquet I will prepare," Esther answered.

Haman was very pleased that the queen had invited him to her banquet. He continued to be in a good mood until he saw Mordecai standing outside the gates of the palace. As usual, Mordecai would not bow to Haman, but this time Haman said nothing to him about it.

When he got home that night, Haman spoke to his wife about all that had happened that day.

"So many things are going well for me," he said. "Yet when I see that Jew, Mordecai, it ruins everything."

Haman's wife suggested that he ask the king for permission to hang Mordecai and get rid of him once and for all. Haman like that idea, and he ordered a gallows built that night.

253. REWARD FOR MORDECAI

Esther 6

Later that night, the king commanded his servant to read to him from the royal record book. The servant came upon the record that told how Mordecai had discovered the two traitors who were going to kill the king.

The king asked Haman the next day what he should do to reward someone who had done a good deed for him. Haman thought the king was talking about him. He told him that he should give the person a royal robe to wear and parade him around town on a horse.

"That's a great idea," the king said. "Take the royal robes out to Mordecai the Jew. He is the one I wish to honor."

Haman could not believe his ears. He ran back to his house to tell his wife that instead of hanging Mordecai, the king wanted to honor him!

Haman's wife warned him that his feud with Mordecai would come to a bitter ending. Just then, a servant arrived to take Haman to Esther's banquet.

254. HAMAN HANGS

Esther 7 - 8

After everyone was seated at Esther's table, enjoying the food and wine she served them, the king leaned over to ask her a question.

"What request can I grant you this evening?" he said.

"Please help my people and me," she said. "There is some-one in your court who wishes to have us all killed."

"Who are you talking about?" the king asked.

The queen pointed to Haman and said, "He is our enemy."

A servant reminded the king that Haman had built a gal-lows to hang Mordecai. The king ordered Haman to hang on it instead.

Even though Haman was dead, the evil law he had written was still in effect. Esther pleaded with the king to change the law. He wanted to do as Esther asked, but in those days any law that the king had signed could not be changed.

"Then write another law making it legal for the Jews to

fight against their attackers," Esther said.

A new law was written and when the day came for the Jews to be killed, they were able to defend themselves in a fair battle.

255. GOD'S FAITHFUL SERVANT

Job 1

Throughout the Bible there are many good men and women who followed God's word and kept his laws no matter what happened. Job was one of these people. He continued to serve God even though many terrible things happened to him.

Job was thankful to God for all he had received. He got up early every day to offer a sacrifice to God before he went to work. Then all through the day, he would stop to whisper a prayer, not for himself, but for his family.

One day the evil Satan came before God. He had been traveling around the earth looking for someone he could tempt into doing something wrong.

"You may as well forget about my servant Job," God said to him. "He only does what is good, and he turns away from evil."

"No wonder he is so good," Satan said. "Look at all the things you have done for him. If you took away his riches, he wouldn't be so loyal to you."

256. SATAN SENDS TROUBLE

Job 2

God told Satan he could put Job to the test as long as he did not harm him personally. Satan wasted no time. Within a few moments of each other, messengers showed up to tell Job that all his flocks and herds had been destroyed and his family had all been killed.

Job fell to the ground when he heard the news. But instead of grieving, Job worshiped and prayed to the Lord.

"I came into this earth with nothing, and I will leave with nothing," he said. "The Lord gave me all that I had, and now he has taken it away. I will bless his name."

Satan came again to speak to God and God spoke of how good Job was. "Even after all you did to him, Job has stayed loyal to me," God told him.

"Yes, but he still has his health," Satan said. "Take that away from him, and he will curse you to your face."

Once again, God allowed Satan to test Job so long as he did not kill him. This time Satan caused Job's body to be covered with painful boils from his head to his feet. It was a time of great trouble for a good man.

257. AN INNOCENT MAN

Job 2 - 3

Three of Job's friends heard about all the trouble he was having. They came to visit and bring him comfort. But Job was so sick by then that he couldn't even talk to them. They sat beside him in silence.

After a while, Job began to speak. He told them he wished he had never been born so that he would not have to endure such terrible suffering.

Two of his friends suggested that maybe he had done something wrong along the way and was being punished.

"An innocent man would not be suffering so badly," they said. "But one who has done evil would receive trouble in return."

Job listened to their words, but in his heart, he knew he had done nothing wrong.

"How much longer are you going to go on accusing me?" he asked them. "I thought you were here to comfort me, but you have only made things worse."

258. MANY QUESTIONS

Job 38 – 42

Job's friends had a point. If he was innocent as he believed himself to be, why was God allowing him to suffer like this? He began to ask questions and complain because he couldn't understand why God was treating him so unfairly.

Suddenly, a great storm came up. A big wind whirled out of the clouds and God's voice began to speak from it.

"Who are you who speaks and knows nothing?" God asked. Job began to feel very ashamed as the questions continued.

"Where were you when I created this earth? Were you there when I made the ocean and the clouds above it?"

Job was very sorry for doubting God's will even for a moment. He apologized to the Lord and prayed for forgiveness. Then the Lord forgave him and healed him. In time, Job was given back his family and twice the riches that he had had before, and the Lord blessed him all the days of his life.

259. A PROMISE

Malachi

God sent the prophet Malachi to tell of the coming of a savior for his people. Malachi warned them to prepare for this great savior.

"You have made the Lord weary with all of your questions and doubts," he said. "Then you ask 'Where is the God of judgment?'

"From the very beginning, the people of Israel have broken God's laws. You think that there is no real reason to serve God. But God will one day reward those who serve him and bring punishment to those who did not."

Malachi told the people of Israel to remember God's commandments that Moses had written down.

"Before God judges his people one final time, he will send a savior who will make your hearts pure so that you can stand before God."

260. GABRIEL'S VISIT

Luke 1

Many years passed after the people of Israel came back to Jerusalem, but they still were not free. The Romans had taken over their land and made it part of the Roman Empire. A man called Herod was chosen by the emperor to be king of the Israelite lands.

Zacharias was a priest in the temple. He and his wife, Elizabeth, were good people who followed God's commandments.

They had hoped for a child of their own for many years, but they were getting very old.

Zacharias and the other priests came to the temple one day to take part in the worship service. The priests drew names to see which one would have the duty of burning incense on the altar. When Zacharias's name was called, he stepped into the room where the altar was kept. He was standing next to the altar.

"Don't be afraid," the angel said. "God has heard your prayer. Elizabeth will have a son, and you must call him John."

261. GOD'S MESSENGER

Luke 1

Zacharias listened to the angel continue to tell him about the son he and Elizabeth would have.

"There will be much joy when your son is born," the angel said. "He will have the power to bring the people back to God. They will turn from their evil ways because of him. And he will prepare the people for the coming of their savior."

"How do I know this is true?" Zacharias asked. "My wife and I are too old for this to happen."

"I am the Angel Gabriel who stands in the presence of God," the angel said. "He has sent me to bring his message to you. Now I will make you unable to speak until after the birth of the child because you did not believe what I told you."

When Zacharias came out of the temple, he could not speak a word. Everyone decided that he must have seen a vision. He swung his hands about trying to tell them all that he had seen. Then he went home to tell Elizabeth.

262. SPECIAL NEWS FOR MARY

Luke 1

As the Angel Gabriel had told them, Elizabeth found out that she was going to have a baby. A few months before the baby came, Gabriel made another visit. This time he went to the city in Galilee called Nazareth.

A young woman lived in the city. Her name was Mary. She was engaged to marry a carpenter named Joseph. But Mary was still a virgin. One day Mary was tending to her chores when she heard a voice.

"Don't be afraid, Mary," Gabriel said. "You have been favored by the Lord. You will soon have a child who will be called Jesus. He will be the great savior who everyone has waited for. He will sit on the throne of David in the house of Jacob, and his kingdom will last forever."

"How can that be?" Mary asked. "I am not married."

"The Holy Spirit will come over you, and the power of God will cause this thing to happen. This child will be the Son of God."

263. LEAPING FOR JOY

Luke 1

Mary told the angel that she was God's servant and would do whatever he asked of her. After the angel left her, she thought about all the amazing things he had told her.

Mary left her home a few days later and went to visit her cousin Elizabeth and Zacharias. When Mary entered their home and said hello, Elizabeth felt her baby leap inside of her.

"You are a blessed woman, Mary," Elizabeth said. "You will give birth to the savior. I know because when I spoke your name, I felt my child leap for joy."

Mary poured out her feelings of joy and thanksgiving to Elizabeth.

"My spirit rejoices in the Lord," she said. "He has chosen me, a poor young girl, from all the women in the land. He has done so many great things for me and all my people. He has shown mercy to the hungry and poor and turned away from the proud and rich."

264. THE BIRTH OF JOHN

Luke 1

Three months later, Elizabeth gave birth to a son. Friends and neighbors gathered at Zacharias's home to rejoice with the happy couple. "You must name the child Zacharias after his father," they said.

"No, his name will be John," Elizabeth told them.

"But there is no one in your family by that name," the neighbors argued.

Then Zacharias wrote something down on his writing pad and showed it to them. "His name is John," it said.

Suddenly, Zacharias was able to speak again. The people in the room were frightened when he began to talk to them. He told them that this child would grow up to be the messenger promised by God.

Then they went out to tell the people of the town all that they had seen and heard, and the people were filled with wonder about the little child named John.

265. THE SAVIOR IS BORN

Luke 2

Right before Mary's baby was due, she and Joseph received word that the Roman Emperor, Caesar Augustus, was ordering people to return to their hometown. There they would be counted in a census and made to pay a tax to the emperor.

Joseph was a descendant of King David. David had been born in a town called Bethlehem. It was a week's journey from Nazareth. Joseph knew that Mary should not be traveling in her condition, but he had no choice.

Once they reached Bethlehem, Mary and Joseph went to an inn to get a room for the night. They found that the inn was already full because so many people had come into town for the census.

The only shelter that was still available was in a barn-like place where animals were kept. It wasn't a very pleasant place, but it was better than sleeping in the streets.

During the night, Mary gave birth to a son. She wrapped him up warmly, and since there was no bed to lay him in, she fixed a place for him to sleep in the manger.

266. THE SHEPHERD'S SEARCH

Luke 2

Some shepherds stayed out in the fields that night, looking after their sheep. An angel of God appeared above them in the sky. The whole sky lit up with the glory of God. The shepherds were very frightened by what they saw.

"Don't be afraid," the angel said. "I bring you good news that will bring joy to all of God's people. Today the savior was born in the city of Bethlehem. You will find him wrapped up in warm clothes and lying in a manger."

Suddenly the sky was filled with many angels singing praises to God.

"Glory to God in the highest," they sang. "And on earth let there be peace and good will toward everyone."

Then the angels went back up to heaven. The shepherds took off in a big hurry and searched the city until they found Mary and Joseph and the baby. Once they had seen the child, they started telling everyone about the baby and all that the angels had said about him.

Mary thought about what the shepherds had told her, but she kept her feelings to herself.

267. WISE MEN COME

Matthew 2

Shortly after Jesus was born, three wise men from the East left their homes and started traveling to Jerusalem. They had seen a bright, shiny star in that direction which they took as a signal that the savior had been born.

"Where is this child who has been born as king of the Jews?" they asked. "We want to come and worship him."

King Herod was not pleased by all this news about a new Jewish king. He called in the priests and record-keepers to ask them about these rumors.

"Where is this Christ supposed to be born?" he asked.

"The prophets have written that the birth will take place in Bethlehem," they answered.

The king asked the three wise men when they had first seen the star. Then he sent them to Bethlehem to look for the child.

"When you find him, send word to me so I can come worship him, too," King Herod said.

268. SPECIAL GIFTS

Matthew 2

The wise men followed the star until it appeared to stand still over the place where Jesus lived. They were filled with joy to have found the savior at last.

When the three men went inside the little house that Joseph had built, they saw Jesus with his mother Mary. They fell down on their knees and worshiped them.

The wise men brought many beautiful gifts with them to give Jesus. They had gold and two special spices called frankincense and myrrh.

After they presented their gifts to the savior, they started home. God had told them in a dream that they should not go back by the palace to tell King Herod where they had found Jesus. They obeyed God and helped keep the new baby safe.

269. RUNNING FROM HEROD

Matthew 2

After the wise men left, an angel of the Lord spoke to Joseph in a dream.

"Get up now and take Jesus and his mother to Egypt," the angel said. "Stay there until you hear from me again. Hurry because Herod has his soldiers out looking for Jesus so they can kill him!"

Joseph did not waste any time following the angel's orders. They left that night for Egypt.

King Herod was very angry when he found out that the wise men had tricked him. He had all the children put to death who had been born in Bethlehem at the same time as Jesus.

After Herod died, the angel of the Lord came to Joseph again in a dream.

"Take Mary and Jesus and go back to Israel now," the angel said. "The ones who wanted to harm the young child are dead."

When Joseph got back to Jerusalem, he found out that Herod's son had taken over his father's throne. He was afraid to stay there, so he took the family back to Galilee and made a home in Nazareth.

270. GROWING UP

Luke 2

After Jesus had grown into a healthy young boy, his parents decided he was old enough to go with them to Jerusalem for the Passover. When the feasting was over, they packed to go back to Nazareth.

A large group of people was traveling together, and Mary and Joseph thought Jesus was in the crowd somewhere. They had been gone a whole day before they knew he was missing.

Joseph and Mary rushed back to Jerusalem to look for Jesus. It was three days before they found him. He had been in the temple all that time, talking to the teachers.

A crowd of people had gathered around Jesus, and they were amazed that such a young boy was so smart in the ways of God.

His parents pushed through the crowd to where Jesus was sitting.

"Why did you run off like that?" Mary said. "Your father and I have been worried sick."

"Didn't you know that I would be in my father's house?" Jesus asked.

271. JOHN THE BAPTIZER

Luke 3

John was the son born to Zacharias and Elizabeth. He was to be the messenger to tell the people about the coming of God's savior. Many people already knew that a child had been born who was supposed to be the king of the Jews, but they needed to get ready for Jesus.

John had a lot of work to do. He left the desert where he had stayed for many years and went to the Jordan River. He wore clothes made of camel's hair and leather. He had a special plan for the people who would listen to him speak.

"The kingdom of heaven is almost here," he said. "Be sorry for your sins." Then he baptized them in the water of the river and told them the good news that Jesus was coming soon.

272. RULES TO FOLLOW

Luke 3

Some of the Jews in the crowd who listened to John did not think they needed to be baptized.

"You must be forgiven from your sins, too," John told them. "Don't think that just because you are descended from Abraham, you are saved from God's judgment."

The people asked what it was that they should do. John told them to stop cheating and robbing one another and to share what they had with the poor. The more he talked, the more the people wondered if he might be the savior.

"I baptize you with water, but one who is greater than I am will come. I am not even worthy to tie his shoes!" John told the crowd. "He will baptize you with the Holy Spirit and with fire!"

Many people came to John to be baptized. Word spread about his preaching. People listened to what he had to say and began calling him John the Baptist because of his baptisms.

273. BAPTIZING THE SAVIOR

Matthew 3

Jesus traveled to the Jordan River from Galilee one day because he wanted to be baptized by John. John recognized him at once.

"You should be baptizing me," he said.

"It's best that we do what is right," Jesus said.

He wanted to be baptized just like everyone else because it was God's will for everyone to ask forgiveness of their sins. So

John lowered Jesus' body into the water of the river and blessed him.

Then Jesus rose up from the muddy water, and the sky seemed to open above him. The Spirit of God took on the shape of a dove and flew down from the opening. As it lit on his shoulder, a voice from heaven spoke to him.

"This is my Son," the voice said. "I love him, and I am very pleased with him."

John knew that the voice was God himself. The savior he had been telling everyone about had finally come.

274. SATAN TEMPTS JESUS

Matthew 4

Jesus was led by the Holy Spirit out into the wilderness. He did not eat anything for forty days and nights.

Satan came out to where Jesus was staying. He saw how hungry Jesus was.

"If you're really the Son of God," Satan said to him, "make these stones turn into bread."

"God told us we are not to live by bread alone, but by his word," Jesus said.

Then Satan took Jesus to Jerusalem and sat him on top of the highest part of the temple. "If you're really the Son of God, go ahead and jump off," Satan said.

"Scripture says you are not supposed to test God like that," Jesus said.

Satan brought Jesus up to a very high mountain where he could see all the kingdoms far and wide. "I will give you power over everything you see below," said Satan. "All you have to do is worship me."

"Go away, Satan!" Jesus told him. "It is written in the commandments that we are to worship no one but God!"

Then Satan knew that Jesus could not be tempted, so he went away.

275. FISHERMEN BECOME FOLLOWERS

Mark 1

Jesus learned that John the Baptist had been put in prison. The king didn't like the idea that John was telling people about a new king who would reign over Israel.

John was being held in Galilee, so Jesus left his home headed in that direction. He was walking to the Sea of Galilee when he saw two people he knew. One was Simon, later renamed Peter, and Simon's brother, Andrew. They were throwing their nets in the water, trying to catch some fish.

Jesus yelled to them. "Come with me and I will make you fishers of men instead of fish."

They left their nets and followed Jesus. After they had walked a little farther, Jesus saw two other men called James and John. They were mending fishing nets by their boats. Jesus called to them, too, and they quickly left what they were doing and followed him.

276. A WEDDING

John 2

Jesus' disciples followed him almost everywhere he went. They listened and learned about God from him, so they could help spread the good news to other people.

Mary, Jesus' mother, went with him one day to a wedding being held in the village of Cana. After the ceremony, everyone joined in a big celebration that was like a reception. The host served wine, a custom in those days.

Not long after the party began, the servants discovered they were out of wine. Mary heard them and turned to Jesus. "They have no more wine," she said.

"What can I do, Mother?" Jesus said to her. "It is not yet time for me to do miracles."

But Mary told the servants to do whatever Jesus asked them to do.

277. WATER TURNED TO WINE

John 2

Jesus saw six pots sitting next to the door. They were the pots the Jewish people used to hold water for the purification ceremony before a meal.

"Fill these with water," Jesus told the servants.

When they obeyed, Jesus told them to take a cupful over to the host. The host took the cup to his lips.

"I thought you served the best wine first," he said, "but this is far better than anything else we've drunk this evening."

The disciples were amazed by what they saw. Their teacher had performed a miracle by turning water into wine. Only a few people at the wedding realized what Jesus had done. Soon news of his miracles spread across the land, and people came from far and near to see him.

278. HELP FOR THE SICK

Mark 1

Jesus and the disciples were on their way home from a Jewish place of worship called the synagogue. They stopped by Simon's house and found Simon's mother-in-law had a very bad fever.

Simon asked Jesus to come quickly. As Jesus stood over the woman and took her hand in his, the fever went away. Then the woman got up, went to her kitchen and fixed food for her guests.

Before the day ended, people began bringing their sick relatives and friends to Jesus for healing. Jesus put his hands on them while he spoke. He made them well and drove the evil spirits out of their bodies.

Later, Jesus went into the cities to preach and heal the sick. A leper in the crowd came up to him. "If you will, you can take away my illness," he said.

Jesus took pity on the man. He touched him and the leprosy was gone. Jesus told the man not to tell anyone what had happened. But the man was so filled with joy that he told everyone he met about the wonderful thing Jesus did for him.

279. THE PEOPLE COME TO JESUS

Mark 2

No matter where Jesus went, the people found out where he was and crowded around him. One night he was staying at a small house in Capernaum. As soon as people learned Jesus was in town, they filled the house and formed a line outside.

Some men brought their friend to see Jesus. The man could not walk, so they carried him on a stretcher. When they saw the lines of people waiting to see Jesus, they knew it would be impossible to get through the crowd.

The four men lifted their friend onto the roof and removed some roofing to make a hole. Then they lowered the stretcher down where Jesus sat. When Jesus saw their great faith, he spoke to the sick man. "Son, your sins are forgiven."

Jesus told the man to get up from his stretcher. "Take your bed with you and go on your way," he said. The man got up immediately and everyone was amazed at how well he could walk.

280. HELP FOR SINNERS

Mark 2

As Jesus traveled the country, preaching God's word, he gathered disciples to follow him. One day Jesus passed by a table where a tax collector named Levi was sitting. Jesus told him to get up and follow him.

Levi, later known as Matthew, was very joyful to be chosen to follow Jesus. He planned a big feast to celebrate.

Lots of people from all over the area arrived at the feast. Not all of them were people who obeyed the law. When the religious leaders saw Jesus eating at the same table with sinners, they were not pleased.

"Why does he sit at the same table with these bad people?" the leaders asked Jesus' disciples.

Jesus heard them talking and answered, "People who are not sick don't need a doctor. I haven't come here to help the good people. I have come to save the sinners."

281. HEALING ON THE SABBATH

Mark 3

One of God's commandments says his people are to rest on the sabbath day and keep it holy. The religious leaders were very careful to follow this rule.

One day Jesus went to the synagogue and found a man there with a terribly crippled hand. Jesus called for the man to come to him.

"What does the law of God tell us we should do on the sabbath day—help people or do harm to them?" Jesus asked the religious leaders. "Should we make people better or let them die?"

Jesus watched the leaders as he spoke. He knew that they considered healing someone to be a form of work just like fixing a fence.

"Put your hand out," Jesus said to the crippled man.

The man's hand was as good as new. He was very pleased, but the leaders were not. They decided that they must find a way to get rid of Jesus.

282. BORN AGAIN

John 3

The religious leaders who did not approve of Jesus were called Pharisees. They liked to keep themselves apart from the others. One of their leaders was Nicodemus.

One night Nicodemus came to talk to Jesus. "We know that God is with you because you perform many miracles," Nicodemus said.

"No one can be with God unless he has been born again," Jesus said.

Nicodemus was puzzled. "But how can a man who is already grown up go back inside his mother and be born again."

Jesus answered, "The body is born from the mother, but the spirit is born of the Holy Spirit. You can't see it happen like you see birth of the body, but the Lord knows when it happens."

"How does this happen?" Nicodemus asked.

"Aren't you a religious teacher?" Jesus asked. "You should know what I'm talking about. I speak about things that you religious leaders do not understand."

283. GOD'S GIFT TO THE WORLD

John 3

Nicodemus was very confused by what Jesus told him. Still, Jesus continued to tell him why God has sent him to earth and what people must do to be saved from their sins.

"No one on earth has been to heaven except the Son of God who came down from heaven. Remember the brass serpent that Moses put up for the people of Israel. Those who looked at the snake as Moses told them to do were healed. That is the way it will be for those who believe in the Son of God. They will be saved.

"For God loves the world so much that he sent his only son, so that whoever believes in him will not die but have eternal life."

Jesus also described himself as a light that had been sent to shine on the earth.

"Men loved the darkness because they could get away with their bad deeds," he said. "But now a light has come to shine on everyone. Those who still do bad things will turn away from the light because they don't want to be seen. But those who do good will want the light to shine on them so their goodness can be seen."

284. THE WATER OF LIFE

John 4

J esus and the disciples were traveling through Samaria one hot day when they reached a well. The disciples went into the city, but Jesus stayed behind to rest. Soon a Samaritan woman came along, carrying pots to draw water.

"May I have a drink of water?" Jesus asked her.

The woman was very surprised that he asked her for water. Jesus was a Jew and Jews did not normally talk to Samaritans.

"If you knew who you were talking to, you would want me to give you a drink of my water," Jesus said.

The woman laughed because Jesus had no pots of water with him.

"The kind of water I give brings eternal life," Jesus told her. "You would never be thirsty again."

The woman said she would like some of that water, so Jesus told her to bring her husband to the well.

"I have no husband," she said.

Jesus told the woman that she had had five husbands and was living with someone else now. The woman was surprised because what Jesus told her was true. She ran home to tell everyone she had met the real Messiah.

285. HELP FOR A SICK BOY

John 4

After Jesus had rested and eaten, he and the disciples continued their trip to Galilee. They were passing through the village of Cana when a nobleman stopped him.

"Please sir. My son needs help. He is sick and I am afraid he will soon die," the man said.

Jesus knew the man must have heard about the miracle he performed at the wedding in Cana. Surely, he expected to see some miracle or sign before he could believe Jesus. The man asked for nothing except for his son.

"Go back to your house," Jesus said. "Your son is alive."

Before he got home, the nobleman's servants met him on the road to tell him the wonderful news—his son was well.

"What time did this happen?" asked the man.

The servants told him, and he knew it was exactly the same time he had been talking to Jesus. Because he believed in Jesus, his son was healed.

286. JOHN IS ARRESTED

Mark 6

Kings had much power when Jesus lived. They did almost anything they wanted. King Herod had taken his own brother's wife for himself. Her name was Herodias.

John the Baptist knew it was against God's laws to take another man's wife. He told Herod that he should not have done this. The king was angry, but not as angry as Herodias. She thought John should be killed for criticizing her marriage to the king.

King Herod knew in his heart that John was a good man. He didn't kill him, but put him in prison instead.

Sometime later, Herod planned a great party to celebrate his birthday. Herodias's daughter, Salome, was brought out to dance for the king. She was a very good dancer. When she finished dancing, the king asked what reward he could give her.

Salome ran to speak with her mother, and then came back.

"I would like you to give me the head of John the Baptist on a plate," she said.

Herod did not want to kill John, but he could not break a promise in front of so many people. He ordered John killed.

287. PREACHING FROM A MOUNTAIN

Matthew 5, Luke 6

Jesus chose twelve disciples to follow him and learn about his teachings. They were: Matthew, the tax collector, Peter, the fisherman, Andrew, John, Bartholomew, Thomas, Thaddaeus, Simon, Philip, Judas Iscariot, and two men, both named James.

Jesus wanted to spend time with the disciples, but so many people wanted to hear him speak that there wasn't a building big enough to hold them. Jesus decided to go up on a mountaintop, so everyone could hear him.

The things Jesus taught the people were different from things the priests taught in the synagogues. He said it was against God's commandments to kill a person, but it was also evil just to think about killing someone. He told everyone to think and behave kindly toward one another. They must be especially good, so they would set an example for unbelievers.

"The person with a pure heart will be blessed," he said. "That person will see God."

288. A SOLID FOUNDATION

Matthew 7

Jesus told the disciples that some people would criticize them for being his followers. He said they must be kind to people trying to hurt them.

"Treat others the same way you would like to be treated."

When Jesus told a story, he put a message in it so the disciples would understand him better. A story like this was called a parable. Jesus told a parable about two houses.

"The man who believes in me is like the man who dug a deep foundation for his house. When the floods came and shook the house, it stood firm," he said.

"But if a man hears me and does not believe me, he is like the man who built his house on top of the earth. He had no foundation, so when the floods came, his house washed away."

He wanted the disciples to understand how important it was for them to have a solid foundation in God's laws.

289. PARABLE OF THE SEEDS

Mark 4

One day Jesus preached to a crowd by the sea. Many people gathered on shore, so he went on board a ship. He spoke to the crowd from out in the water, telling them a parable about seeds.

"A man went out to plant seeds in his garden. Some seeds fell on rocks and the birds ate them. Other seeds fell on shallow soil. They sprouted but didn't live long.

"Some seeds fell in weeds, and their growth was choked out. But other seeds landed on rich, pure soil. Those seeds grew into many healthy plants."

The people wondered what Jesus meant by his parable, but the disciples began to understand.

"You are the sowers of God's word," Jesus said to the disciples. "You will spread the word to many people, but only a few will listen. They will become the fruit of God's earth."

290. FAITH THAT GROWS

Matthew 13

Jesus wanted to tell the people about the kingdom of heaven. He chose two parables, one about a mustard seed and another about making bread.

"The kingdom of heaven is like a mustard seed that is planted," Jesus said. "It is the smallest of all seeds, but it grows into a big plant. The herb that comes from it is the greatest of herbs."

Jesus said the kingdom of heaven is also like bread. "A woman takes a small amount of yeast and puts it in her dough. The yeast makes the dough rise up to many times its size. Faith is like yeast. A few faithful followers can spread God's message, and soon there will be many to join God's kingdom."

Then he told a parable about harvesting grain among the weeds.

"Although grain grows alongside weeds, it is easy to tell the good grain from the weeds at harvest time. The grain will be saved, but the weeds will be destroyed."

291. CALMING THE STORM

Mark 4

When Jesus finished telling the people the parables of the seeds and bread, it was evening. He and the disciples decided to stay on the boat and cross the sea to the other side.

Jesus went below the deck to rest. As he slept, a big storm came up. The winds blew water over the decks, and the boat began to fill up.

"Master! Master!" the disciples yelled to Jesus. "We are about to sink!"

Jesus got up from his bed and spoke to the wind and rain.

"Be still," he said. Suddenly, the storm went away.

"Where is your faith?" Jesus asked the disciples.

But the disciples were afraid because of what they had seen Jesus do.

"What kind of man is this?" they said to themselves. "He can tell the winds to be calm and they obey him!"

292. THE WILD MAN

Mark 5

When the boat landed on the other side, Jesus walked out onto the shore. A man had watched the boat from the cave where he lived. He was a wild-looking man who had been driven mad by evil spirits.

Just then the men recognized Jesus walking towards him. He ran to Jesus and fell on the ground before him. A loud voice cried out from deep within him.

"Don't hurt me, Jesus," it said.

Jesus asked the man his name, and he told them, Legions, because he was filled with so many demons.

The demons were very afraid because they knew who Jesus was. They left the man and went over to a herd of grazing pigs. The pigs squealed wildly. They ran over a cliff into the sea where they drowned.

The men who tended the pigs took off for the city to tell people what had happened. A group of people soon came to the shore to see Jesus. They saw the wild man sitting calmly next to Jesus, and were very impressed.

"Let us go with you," they said to Jesus.

But Jesus told them to go back and spread the word about what they had seen.

293. HEALING BY FAITH

Mark 5

A large crowd waited to welcome Jesus back from his trip across the Sea of Galilee. When he greeted them, a man pushed through the people and fell at Jesus' feet. His name was Jairus. He was a leader in the synagogue.

"Please come see my daughter," he begged. "I'm afraid she is dying."

Jesus followed the man back to his house. Many people crowded around them as they walked by, but suddenly Jesus felt he had been touched by someone.

"Who touched me?" he said. His disciples answered that many people had reached out to touch him.

"But I feel that some of my healing strength has left my body," Jesus told them.

Then a woman appeared from the crowd and told Jesus that she touched him because she was very sick. As soon as she touched his coat, she felt well again.

"Go now and live in comfort," Jesus said to her. "Because you have faith in me, you are healed."

294. AWOKEN FROM SLEEP

Mark 5

While Jesus talked to the woman who touched his coat, two messengers from Jairus's home came up to them.

"You do not need to bring Jesus to your house, Jairus," they said. "Your daughter is dead."

Jairus was very upset. The little girl, his only daughter, was just twelve years old.

Jesus heard what the messengers said. He told Jairus, "Don't be afraid. Keep believing, and your daughter will be all right."

When they reaching Jairus's house, Jesus took Peter, James, and John with him to the girl's room. The mother sat crying by her daughter's side.

"Don't cry," Jesus said. "The girl is not dead. She is only sleeping."

They laughed at Jesus because everyone knew the girl was dead. So Jesus told them all to leave and took the girl's hand and told her to get up.

The parents could not believe their eyes. Their daughter got up from bed, and Jesus asked them to get her some food.

295. TWO BLIND MEN

Matthew 9

Jesus and the disciples left Jairus's house to go back out among the crowd. Two blind men were following Jesus. They begged him to have mercy on them because they could not see.

"Do you believe I can give you back your sight?" Jesus asked them. When they answered yes, he touched their eyes, and both men were able to see again.

Jesus didn't want the word to spread about the great miracles he was able to do. He told Jairus, his wife, and the two blind men not to tell anyone what he had done for them. That did not stop them from telling the story all over town. Soon the Jewish leaders called Pharisees heard about Jesus' miracles.

One day a group of people were talking about the way Jesus chased away an evil spirit from a man who could not speak. He got his voice back and was able to speak.

"If he can talk to demons and scare them away, then he must be a demon himself," the Pharisees said.

296. SINS FORGIVEN

Luke 7

The Pharisees always tried to find fault with Jesus. They were jealous of the powers he claimed to have.

A Pharisee named Simon invited Jesus to his home for dinner one evening. A woman who had committed many sins found out where Jesus was eating and came to Simon's house.

The Pharisee said nothing as he watched the woman sit before Jesus' feet. She cried many tears and wiped them up with her hair. Then she kissed Jesus' feet and put a sweet smelling oil on them.

"This man can't be a prophet," Simon thought to himself. "If he were, he would know that this woman is a sinner and he would have nothing to do with her."

Jesus knew what the man was thinking. He asked Simon a question about repaying debts.

"A man loaned one man a lot of money and another man only a little and told both of them they didn't have to pay him back. Which one of the men would love him the most?"

Simon said the one who had been loaned the most money. Jesus told him that he was forgiving the woman's sins because she showed him more love and respect than Simon did.

297. MERCY FOR THE WIDOW'S SON

Luke 7

While going through the town of Nain one day, Jesus and his followers were stopped at the gates by a passing funeral procession.

The people mourned and cried as they watched the body of a young man being carried by. They knew the woman walking next to the body was a widow who had lost both her husband, and now, her only son.

Jesus took pity on the poor, sad woman.

"Don't cry," he said.

The men carrying the body stood still as Jesus came over and touched the corpse.

"Get up, young man," he said.

The boy got up and began to speak out loud. Jesus picked him up and handed him to his mother.

Everyone was frightened by what they had seen.

"This must be the great prophet God promised to send us," they said. So they went about the country telling everyone the good news about Jesus.

298. SPREADING THE WORD

Luke 9

The disciples had followed Jesus for a long time. They had heard him preach, seen his miracles, and learned the lessons he taught them. Now they were ready to go out on their own and spread the good news of God's forgiveness through the savior.

Jesus gave the disciples instructions before they went on their journey.

"Don't take anything with you except a loaf of bread," he said. "You won't need any extra clothes or money."

He told them to go to each house along the way.

"If they let you in, go in and tell them everything I have told you about being born again into God's kingdom. But if you go to a place and they will not let you in, wipe the dust off your feet as a sign to them that God has brushed them off."

Then Jesus sent the disciples out, two by two, into the land. They each had the same kind of powers Jesus had to call out evil spirits and heal the sick. So they were able to help Jesus in all his work.

299. THE FIVE THOUSAND

Mark 6

When the disciples returned from their journey, they were anxious to tell Jesus about what they had seen and done. They looked for a quiet place to meet and talk, but the people soon found out where they were hiding. By the day's end, nearly five thousand people had arrived to hear Jesus!

No one had eaten, and the disciples were hungry.

"Let's send everyone away, so we can eat dinner," they said.

Jesus told them to feed the crowd whatever food they had.

"But we only have two fish and five loaves of bread," they argued. "That won't feed many people."

"Make them sit down in groups of fifty," Jesus instructed.

The disciples did as Jesus asked. Then Jesus took the bread and fish and raised them up. He said a prayer, blessed the food, and broke it into pieces.

The disciples passed out the food to the people, and everyone ate plenty. There was even some left over!

300. A WALK ON THE WATER

Mark 6

After the huge dinner was over, many people crowded around Jesus to thank him for feeding them. Jesus knew the disciples were tired, so he sent them on ahead to the boat. The disciples waited for Jesus to join them down by the Sea of Galilee.

Jesus stopped to pray on a mountaintop. He thanked God for what had happened that day. Meanwhile, the disciples grew tired of waiting and took off in the boat. A storm came up suddenly, and the wind steered the boat off course. Jesus could see his friends were in trouble. He stepped out into the water, but instead of sinking, he walked across the water to the boat.

The disciples saw him coming and thought they were seeing a ghost.

"If that is you, Lord," Peter yelled, "let me come to you."

Peter walked out of the boat and onto the water as well, but he became very scared and began to sink.

"Help me, Lord!" he cried.

Jesus held out his hand to lift Peter up from the water.

"Where is your faith, Peter?" he said, leading him back to the boat.

301. HELP FOR EVERYONE

Matthew 15

A woman from the land of Canaan stopped Jesus and the disciples as they traveled to the cities of Tyre and Sidon.

She was crying, and said to Jesus, "Son of David, please have mercy on me. My daughter is very sick, and I'm afraid she will die."

The disciples begged Jesus to turn her away. "She is following us and making too much noise."

Then Jesus spoke to her. "I have come only to help the lost people of Israel. You are not one of these people."

The woman kneeled at Jesus' feet. "Please help me, sir."

Jesus said, "It is not right to take the food that belongs to my children and throw it to the dogs."

"Yes, that is true, sir," said the woman, "but even dogs are happy to eat the leftovers from their master's table."

Jesus said to her, "You have much faith. The thing you want will be given to you." At that moment, the woman's little girl was healed.

302. SEEING AND HEARING

Mark 7

A fter Jesus left the city, he went back down to the Sea of Galilee. As he passed through a group of villages, some people brought him a deaf and dumb man to be healed. The man could not hear anything, and his speech was so bad that he could hardly be understood by others.

Jesus took the man aside and touched his ears and tongue. Then Jesus looked up to heaven and said, "Be opened."

Immediately, the man's hearing came back. He opened his mouth to speak, and the words came easily to him. Returning to the crowd, he spoke loudly about the miracle Jesus had done.

"Please, I ask all of you not to tell anyone what has happened here today," Jesus said.

But the more Jesus protested, the more the people insisted that everyone should know about the man who could perform miracles.

"He can do anything," the people said about Jesus. "He can make the deaf hear and the dumb speak."

303. WALKING TREES

Mark 8

Another large crowd gathered to hear Jesus speak. This time the disciples had only brought seven loaves of bread and two fish. But Jesus broke them into pieces as he had done before, and all four thousand people who were there got something to eat.

Jesus' popularity spread among the people. Everywhere he went, someone came up to him for healing or for a blessing. One time some people brought their blind friend to Jesus for help.

Jesus led the blind man away from the crowd. He put his hands over the man's eyes. Jesus asked him what he saw.

"I see men that look like trees walking around," he said.

Again Jesus touched the man's eyes. This time he told the man to look up in the sky. When he looked down again, he could see everything clearly.

"Go back to your home now," Jesus said to the man. "Don't stop to tell anyone in town about what has happened to you."

304. WHO AM I?

Mark 8

Everyone who heard about Jesus knew that he was a great man with special powers. Jesus wanted them to understand his message, but he feared that if the priests and leaders of the government found out who he was, they would want to kill him right away.

"Who do the people think I am?" Jesus asked his disciples one day.

"Well, some of them think that you are John the Baptist come back from the dead," they said. "Also, they say you could be the prophet Elijah, or another of the prophets.

"But who do you think I am?" Jesus asked them.

Peter spoke up immediately. "You are Christ, the Son of God!"

Jesus was glad that his disciples knew who he really was. He told them not to tell everyone else though.

"There are many things I must do before I leave this world," he said. "I will suffer many things, and when I am killed, I will come back to life after three days. That is the way God has planned it."

305. FOLLOWING CHRIST

Mark 8

As Peter listened to Jesus talk about leaving them, he became very upset. "We don't want you to be killed," he said. "Please do not tell us such terrible things."

"You are talking like Satan," Jesus said. "That's the kind of thing he would say to keep me from doing God's will."

Jesus called the crowd to come closer, so they could hear what he had to say.

"If you want to follow me, you must give up the way of life you're living now," he said. "Anyone who wants to go his own way will not see the kingdom of heaven. But those who leave their life behind to follow me will be rewarded with a place in heaven when they die.

"If you are ashamed to follow me in this life, I will be ashamed of you when you come to the gates of heaven," Jesus continued. "Don't think too much about this world. It is better to leave the ways of the world behind and save your soul than lose your soul to the sins of the world."

306. A VISION FROM HEAVEN

Mark 9

Jesus took James, John, and Peter with him to the top of a nearby mountain. He wanted only these three disciples to see what he had to show them.

Once they were alone, Jesus began to change in front of them. Suddenly, his clothes shone like a bright, white light. Next to him stood two people. The three disciples could tell that the two people were Moses and Elijah. That was very frightening to them because Moses and Elijah had been dead for many years.

Peter spoke up, asking Jesus if he should set up three tents for Jesus and his visitors.

Just then, a cloud formed overhead, and a voice spoke.

"This is my Son," it said. "Listen to him."

The disciples looked down again and saw that the angels of Moses and Elijah had disappeared. Only Jesus stood there, looking as he had before they came up the mountain. He told them not to tell anyone about what they had seen until the time came for him to rise from the dead.

307. A DOUBTING MAN

Mark 9

Many people were waiting for Jesus and the three disciples to come down from the mountain. A man who had brought his son to be healed stepped forward.

"Please help my son," the man said to Jesus. "He has an evil spirit in him that makes him thrash around on the floor and grit his teeth. Sometimes foam comes from his mouth like an animal. I asked your disciples to heal him, but they could not get rid of the spirit."

"You faithless people," Jesus said to him. "How long will I have to put up with you?"

They brought the son to Jesus, but when he saw Jesus the boy fell to the floor in another fit. Jesus asked the father how long the child had been ill. The man answered that his son had been having fits all of his life. "Please help us if you can," the father said.

"All things are possible to those who believe," Jesus said.

"I believe you, Lord," the man said. "Forgive me for doubting you."

So Jesus chased away the evil spirit, calming the boy.

308. WHO'S THE GREATEST?

Mark 9

The disciples were special men because Jesus chose them to follow him and study his teachings. But they still had faults just like any other men. They got into an argument on the way to preach in another town.

Jesus knew what was on their minds, but he asked them what they were talking about anyway. No one answered him.

"I know that you were thinking about which one of you is the greatest disciple," he said. "Let me tell you something. If any one of you wants to be first, you must be willing to be last. Only the one who serves others before himself will be thought of as great."

Jesus lifted up a child from the crowd. He held the child in his arms as he spoke.

"Whoever welcomes a child into his home and heart welcomes me, too," Jesus told them. "If you welcome me into your life, you welcome my father, also."

309. THE FIRST COME LAST

Matthew 20

Jesus told his disciples another story to explain how people who seemed to be last would come first in God's eyes.

"A man who owned a big house and a farm hired some workers for the day," Jesus said. "He soon found some men willing to work at his vineyard for one penny a day.

"Later, he found more men who wanted to work. Just before the day was through, he saw other men standing around and asked them why they were not working. "No one has hired us," they said. So the man told them to go back to his vineyard and work with the others.

"When the men came to be paid at the day's end, the man gave them all the same amount of money. Some of the men were very unhappy because they had worked many hours for their pay, while the others hadn't worked long at all. The man said that he had been fair to them all because each man had agreed to work for the pay.

"That is the way it is in the kingdom of heaven," Jesus said. "Those who come first will be last and the last ones will be treated as if they were the first."

310. A GOOD SAMARITAN

Luke 10

A teacher of the law asked Jesus, "What must I do to get to heaven?"

Jesus said, "What does the Bible tell you?"

"That you must love the Lord and love your neighbor," answered the teacher.

"You are right," said Jesus.

"But who is our neighbor?" asked the teacher.

Jesus told him this story:

"Robbers attacked a man traveling from Jerusalem to the town of Jericho. They beat him and stole his money. A priest came by shortly after, but he pretended not to see the injured man. Another person came along, looked at the man, but walked away. Then a Samaritan discovered the man, and stopped to help him. He carried him to an inn and cared for him."

Jesus asked the teacher which of these three men acted like a neighbor to the man who was hurt.

"The one who stopped to help him," said the teacher.

"Then that is what you must do," said Jesus.

311. A SPECIAL PRAYER

Luke 11

Jesus often went off by himself to pray. One time when he came back where the disciples were staying, they asked him to teach them a prayer.

"When you pray to God, this is what you must say," Jesus told them. "Our Father who is in heaven, we honor your name. We pray that your kingdom will come soon. We want to do your will on earth, the same as it is done in heaven.

"Please give us the food we need each day. Forgive our sins, the same way that we forgive others for hurting us. Keep us away from temptation, but save us from evil if we do wrong.

"For yours is the kingdom of power and glory that will go on forever and ever."

Jesus told his disciples to always say their prayers in private.

"Don't be like the hypocrites who pray in public so everyone will see them," he said. "Pray to God in secret, and if you are sincere and do not doubt him, he will reward you openly."

312. A KNOCK ON THE DOOR

Luke 11

After Jesus taught the disciples his special prayer, he wanted them to know that God really listened to them when they prayed. Even if they prayed for something for a long time and nothing happened, they were not to give up.

"What if you go to your friend after midnight and ask to borrow three loaves of bread?" he said. "What do you think he will say?"

"You may tell him that you need the bread to feed a friend who has stopped by unexpectedly. But he will probably just tell you to go away and come back tomorrow.

"If you stay there, knocking on his door, sooner or later he will come out and give you what you need."

Jesus told the disciples to keep praying to God. "Ask God for what you need, and he will give it to you," he said. "If you keep knocking long enough at his door, eventually he will open it to you."

313. GOD WILL PROVIDE

Luke 12

A group of people stood around one day, listening to Jesus speak. He told them a parable about riches.

"A rich farmer produced many crops on his farm one year," Jesus said. "He decided to build huge barns to hold it all. That way he could store up enough food for many seasons, so he wouldn't have to work on his farm anymore.

"That night God spoke to him in a dream. He told the rich man that he would die in his sleep. 'You foolish man,' God said to him. 'What good will all your riches do you now?'"

Jesus told his disciples not to worry about what they would eat or wear.

"Birds don't plant seeds and harvest crops," he said. "God provides food for them. Surely, you are more important in God's eyes than the birds.

"The lilies in the fields don't sew or spin yarn, but they are dressed finer than any king. If God clothes the flowers and grass so well, think how much better he will clothe you."

314. GIVING UP POSSESSIONS

Mark 10

A man had an important question to ask Jesus. He came running up to him and fell down on his knees.

"Good teacher, what must I do to have eternal life?" he asked.

"You know what the commandments are," Jesus said to him. "Do not commit adultery, don't kill or steal, don't lie or cheat, and show honor for your mother and father."

The man shook his head eagerly. "Yes, teacher. I have kept all these commandments since I was young."

Jesus looked at the man. He felt love and kindness for him because he was a good man.

"There is one thing you must do," Jesus told him. "You must sell all that you own and give the money to the poor. Then you can follow me and have a great treasure waiting for you in heaven."

The man was sad because he was very rich and had many possessions. He turned away from Jesus and went on his way.

315. A GREAT GIFT

Mark 10, 12

The disciples were amazed by what Jesus told them about riches. He said that it was very hard for a rich man to have eternal life. "It is easier for a camel to go through the eye of a needle, than it is for a rich man to enter God's kingdom."

Jesus sat with his disciples near the temple's entrance. They watched people pass by and place money in the collection plate. Many rich people came by and tossed in handfuls of gold coins.

A poor old woman placed two small coins in the plate. Jesus called his disciples over to him.

"That poor widow has put more into the plate than all the other people put together," he said.

Jesus saw that his disciples did not understand him, so he explained what he meant.

"Those rich people put in only a little of their great wealth," he said. "But that woman put in all she had. To her, God is more important than money."

316. A TREE WITH NO FRUIT

Luke 13

People had many chances to follow Jesus. He and his disciples travelled all over the land, spreading the message of salvation. Many people, like the rich man, did not want to give up their possessions and way of life. Jesus told them that they must turn away from their sins or they would be lost forever.

"Consider the man who had a fig tree in his grove," Jesus said. "He kept coming back to see if it had any figs on it. But each time he found none.

"One day he told the gardener that he was tired of waiting for the tree to produce fruit like it was supposed to do. 'Go ahead and cut it down,' he said.

"The gardener begged him to spare the tree for one more year. 'I will give it extra special attention this year,' he said. 'If it doesn't have any fruit on it next year, I'll cut it down.'"

Jesus wanted the people to understand that he was like the gardener. He had come to give them special care, but if they didn't listen to him, they would be destroyed like the fig tree.

317. GOD'S FEAST IN HEAVEN

Luke 14

Some people thought they were very important, not because they were rich, but because of their race. The Jews were God's chosen people, so they certainly thought that they would have a place in God's kingdom.

"A man wanted to have a big feast and invite all his friends," Jesus said to the Pharisees. "He sent his servant out to deliver the invitations. But when the servant went to the houses, the people told him they could not come to his master's party. They had other, more important, things to do.

"The man was very angry that his friends had turned their backs on his invitation. 'I'll have the party without them,' he thought. So he sent his servant out again to find people in the streets and on the roadsides to come to his feast. Most of the people the servant found were sick or poor, but he brought them anyway."

Jesus told the Jewish Pharisees that they must be forgiven of their sins like everyone else. If they refused, someone else would take their place in God's kingdom.

318. THE WORK OF HEALING

Luke 13

Jesus taught that we must love and take care of one another all the time. There are no "days off" when we can turn away from our loved ones and friends.

Jesus was teaching in the synagogue one sabbath day when a woman came in, seeking his help. She was very deformed by an illness she had had for eighteen years. Jesus called her over to him.

"Woman, your deformity is healed," he said.

Then he laid his hands on her. She straightened her back and arms. The woman was filled with thanks and glory to God. She shouted praises to him, but the elders of the synagogue, who had been watching, were not so pleased.

"You know it is not right to work on the sabbath day," they said to Jesus.

"Don't be such a hypocrite," he answered. "Don't you lead your oxen and donkeys out of their stalls on the sabbath so they can get a drink of water? That is work, too. Don't you think healing a person is more important than watering an animal?"

319. HELP FOR A BLIND MAN

John 9

Jesus used his healing powers not only to help people, but also to show how great God's power is. Once as he walked down a road, Jesus came across a blind beggar.

His disciples asked, "Teacher, did this man commit a sin, or did his parents do something wrong to make him be born blind?"

"No, God made him blind for a purpose," Jesus told them. "He will become an example of God's work."

Jesus placed some mud over the beggar's eyes and told him to go to the pool of Siloam and wash it off. When the beggar returned, he was filled with joy and thankfulness because he could see.

Neighbors who knew the beggar were puzzled by what had happened. They weren't sure if the beggar was telling them the truth, or if someone had been made up to look like the beggar to trick them.

"The beggar says a man came by and put clay on his eyes, and he was able to see," they said to one another. "Let's take him to the Pharisees and see what they will say about his story."

320. THE BEGGAR BELIEVES

John 9

The Pharisees asked the beggar to tell his story again and again. They didn't know what to make of it.

"The man who healed the beggar cannot be a man of God because he healed him on a sabbath day," one of them said.

"If he is a sinner, how do you explain the miracle he performed by making this blind man see?" asked another.

The beggar said that the man who healed him must be a prophet, but the Pharisees did not believe him. They asked his parents, who had come with him, what they thought.

"All we know is that our son was born blind, and now he can see," they said.

"You should be giving God credit for this miracle, not this sinner," the Pharisees said. But the beggar continued to defend the man who had given his sight back. Eventually, the Pharisees got disgusted with the beggar and threw him out of the synagogue.

Jesus found the beggar again and asked him if he believed in the Son of God.

"I don't know who he is," the beggar said.

When Jesus told him that he was talking with God's Son, the beggar became very excited. "I believe in you," he said.

321. A SHEPHERD AMONG MEN

John 10

Jesus knew that the really good people who knew and loved him would eagerly follow him. Although they might be blind like the beggar, they would recognize who he was when he came to them.

"If a man goes into the sheep's stall at night, but doesn't use the door, you know he must be a thief," Jesus told the people.

"But if a man comes through the door, then you know that man is the shepherd. The sheep hear and recognize his voice. He can call all his sheep by name, and they follow him.

"They will not follow a stranger, because they don't know his voice. They will become scared and run away."

Jesus told the people that he was their shepherd. He would stand by the door and keep out all the robbers and thieves.

"I am like a good shepherd who would lay down his life for his flock," Jesus said. "I will call out to my sheep, and if another lamb hears and recognizes my voice, even though he is not part of my flock, I will welcome and care for him, too."

322. LOST SHEEP

Luke 15

One day Jesus spoke to a crowd of people who had done many bad things. Other religious people in towns became angry at Jesus. They said, "Look, he welcomes these bad people and even sits down to eat with them."

Jesus said to the townspeople:

"What do you do if you are tending one hundred sheep and you see that one of them is missing? You leave the herd of ninety-nine and go looking for the lost sheep. When you find it, you are very happy. You carry it back home with you and say 'Look! I have found my lost sheep. Let us celebrate!'

"That is how God feels when a sinner comes to ask him for forgiveness. He is happy to have ninety-nine good people who follow him, but he is more happy to find the one person he lost."

323. LOOKING FOR A COIN

Luke 15

Jesus told another story about God's joy when a sinner is forgiven and starts to follow God's ways.

"A woman may have ten coins in her purse, but if she loses one of them, she searches the house until she finds it," Jesus said.

"She gets a light and looks behind the furniture. She sweeps the floors in every room of the house.

"When she finds the coin, she is very excited. She calls up all her friends and tells them that her coin is now found.

"It is that way in heaven when a sinner comes to God. The angels rejoice because someone lost in sin has returned to God."

The woman's other nine coins are like all the good people who follow God. They are important, too, but they are never lost. They are always in God's care.

324. TWO SONS

Luke 15

The parable of the runaway son is a story of regret and forgiveness. Jesus told this story to the Pharisees, so they would understand that even people who have done bad things are worthy of God's love.

"A man had two sons. One day the youngest son decided he wanted to go out on his own," Jesus told them. "He asked the father to give him his share of the family inheritance. So the father divided his wealth between the two boys, and the younger one left home for the city.

"Soon the young boy spent everything he had because there were many ways to spend money in the city. He had nothing to show for his money. He had used it all to have a good time.

"The boy took a job tending pigs. He hated the job and he barely made enough money to buy food with. He was hungry every day. He began to think about the servants back on his father's farm. 'At least they get three square meals a day,' he said to himself.

"So he decided to swallow his pride and go back home to his father."

325. COMING HOME

Luke 15

The father missed his son very much," Jesus continued. "When he looked down the road one day and saw his son coming toward him, he ran and kissed him.

"'I have committed many sins, Father,' said the boy. 'I am no longer worthy of your love.'

"But the father would not listen to the boy. He ordered the servants to bring out a fine robe for him and plan a big feast. They would cook up the meat from the fattest calf in the field.

"The older son heard all the commotion and asked what was going on. When he heard that the feast was to honor his brother, he got very angry.

"'I have stayed with you and served you all this time,' he said to his father. 'But you have never rewarded me with such a great feast.'

"The father told him he should be rejoicing at his brother's return. 'Your brother was dead, but now he is alive again,' he said. 'We should be glad that he has found his way back to us.'"

326. A WARNING FROM BELOW

Luke 16

The Pharisees were interested in money. They liked to show off on the outside, but Jesus knew what was really in their hearts. He told them a story about a rich man and a beggar to show that God's forgiveness is important, no matter how much money a person has.

"Once a rich man had every comfort a man could desire," Jesus said. "Outside the gates of his beautiful home was a sick beggar who had nothing to eat.

"Both men died in time, and the beggar went to heaven. The rich man went to a place called hell. It was a terrible place and the rich man was very, very miserable. He could see the beggar up in heaven, resting comfortably.

"'Please let the beggar come down here and touch some cool water to my tongue,' he said. 'I am burning in fire.'

"Abraham heard the man, for he was up in heaven with the beggar. 'You had comforts while you lived, and this man had none. Now things are the opposite,' he said.

"The man begged Abraham to send someone back from the dead to warn the people on earth."

Jesus ended the story by saying that if they don't believe God's word now, sending someone back from the dead won't help them.

327. FORGIVENESS AMONG MEN

Matthew 18

When Jesus taught his disciples to pray, he told them to ask God to forgive them as they forgave each other. Sometimes it is hard to be forgiving, but Jesus told a story to show how important it is.

"A king was looking through his accounts one day and discovered that one certain servant owed him a lot of money. He called in his guards and told them to sell the servant and his family as slaves.

"The servant came running to the king and fell down on his knees in front of him. 'Please be patient with me,' he cried. 'I will pay you back.'

"The king let him go. As he left, the servant bumped into someone who owed him money. He told the man to pay back the money right away, or he would have him sent to prison.

"The other servants found out what happened and told the king. 'How dare you throw that man in prison for being in your debt, after I just forgave you your debts,' said the king. Then he threw the servant in prison to punish him."

328. THE LITTLE CHILDREN

Mark 10

People had many wrong ideas about what it took for them to enter the kingdom of heaven. The rich thought they were important, but Jesus told them the poor would be more welcome in God's kingdom. The Jews thought they were the people God had chosen to be with him in heaven. Jesus taught that anyone who confesses his sins and begins to follow God's ways will be with God.

Once while Jesus talked to a group of people, some women brought their children to the place where Jesus was sitting. They wanted Jesus to bless their children by touching them.

The disciple told the women to move back. They thought the children were disturbing Jesus.

Jesus stopped the disciples right away. "Let the children come to me," he said. "God's kingdom is made up of his children. Unless someone comes to God as a child does, trusting and believing in him, he will never enter the kingdom of heaven." He then took the disciples in his arms, put his hands on them, and blessed them.

329. A THANK YOU

Luke 17

Ten men who had a skin disease called leprosy saw Jesus walking down the road. They knew he could heal people because everyone in the village talked about the many wonderful things Jesus had done.

"Please help us, master," they said.

The people following Jesus backed away when the lepers came toward him. They believed leprosy was contagious. Jesus was not afraid of the men. He felt pity for them.

"Go show yourselves to the priests," he told the lepers.

The men went to the priests who said they were cured. All the men were very happy. Now they could go back and live with their families. Only one man returned to thank Jesus.

"Didn't I heal ten men?" Jesus asked. "What happened to the other nine?"

Jesus reached out his hand to the Samaritan man. "Get up and go your way," he said. "Your faith has made you well."

330. A SICK FRIEND

John 11

Jesus had some good friends living in the town of Bethany. They were named Mary, Martha, and Lazarus. He had met Mary when she came to the Pharisees' dinner party uninvited and wiped Jesus' feet with her hair. Jesus had forgiven Mary of her sins, and he often visited with her and her sister, Martha and their brother, Lazarus.

Mary and Martha sent for Jesus to come quickly one day because Lazarus had become very sick. When Jesus got the message, he said to his disciples, "Lazarus will not die. He is sick for a purpose sent from God."

So Jesus did not go to Bethany for two more days. He told the disciples that Lazarus had fallen asleep, and they must go wake him now.

"If he's sleeping, that must mean he will soon be well," the disciples answered.

"I meant Lazarus is dead," Jesus said. "I'm glad we weren't there when it happened, so you will believe in me when you see what I do. Now let us go to him."

331. MARTHA'S FAITH

John 11

The disciples didn't understand what Jesus meant when he talked about Lazarus. But still they followed Jesus to Bethany. When they got there, they found out Lazarus was already buried.

"Jesus, if you had only been here, my brother would still be alive," Martha said to Jesus. "But I know that even now if you ask God for anything, he will give it to you."

Then Jesus said to her, "Your brother will live again."

"Yes, I know he will live again on the resurrection day," she said.

"I am the resurrection," Jesus said to her. "Anyone who believes in me, even though he might die, will live again. Do you believe in me, Martha?"

"I believe you are Christ, the Son of God," Martha said.

Martha left quickly to tell Mary that Jesus had come and wanted to see her. Mary tried to be quiet, so the other Jews who had come to mourn Lazarus would not know what was going on. They heard Mary get up and leave in the night, and thinking she was going to Lazarus's grave, they followed her.

332. LAZARUS LIVES

John 11

By the time Mary and the others reached Lazarus's grave, they were crying because they were so sad. Jesus saw how much pain they felt, and he began crying, too.

The Jews who were with Mary knew of all the miracles Jesus had done. They wondered whether he could have saved Lazarus if he had gotten there before Lazarus died. While they stood around, Jesus told some of them to move the stone lying in front of Lazarus's grave. When they did, Jesus looked up to the sky and said a prayer.

"Thank you for hearing me, Father," he said. "Now may the people hear me and know you have sent me."

Then Jesus surprised everyone by calling out to Lazarus.

"Come out, Lazarus," he yelled. And Lazarus came out, still wrapped in the clothing they had buried him in.

The people were amazed by such a great miracle. Many began to believe Jesus really was the Son of God. Others were frightened by what they saw. They ran to the Pharisees to tell them that they had seen Jesus bring a dead man back to life.

333. A PRECIOUS GIFT

John 12

Soon it was time for the Passover Feast to begin. Jesus and his disciples started their journey to Jerusalem. They stopped again in Bethany to see Mary, Martha, and Lazarus. Martha served a big meal for everyone. They were happy to be together once more.

Mary brought out expensive perfume she had been saving. She broke open the perfume's container and poured some of it on Jesus' head. Then she spilled the perfume on his feet and wiped them with her hair.

"Why have you done such a thing?" Judas, the disciple, asked. "We could have sold that perfume and given the money to the poor."

"Leave her alone," Jesus told him. "The poor will always be with you, but I will soon be gone."

Jesus knew Mary had kept the perfume as a gift, and he was very thankful. His friends' kindness meant a great deal to him now because he knew he faced a terrible death.

334. BLIND BARTIMAEUS

Mark 10

Traveling to Jerusalem, Jesus and the disciples passed through the town of Jericho. A blind man named Bartimaeus lived on the edge of town. Each day he sat by the side of the road, begging for food and money.

A crowd of people gathered around Jesus to hear his stories and parables. As they shouted out Jesus' name, Bartimaeus heard them. He knew who Jesus was because he heard people talk about the miracles Jesus had performed. If only he could get Jesus' attention, Bartimaeus believed Jesus would cure him of his blindness.

"Jesus, Jesus," he shouted. "Please have pity on me."

The people yelled at Bartimaeus to be quiet. But Jesus heard the blind man and told him to come forward. Bartimaeus let his robe fall to the ground and walked toward the spot where he heard Jesus' voice.

"What can I do for you?" Jesus asked him.

"Lord, I want to see," Bartimaeus said.

Jesus told Bartimaeus that because he believed in him, he would see again. Immediately Bartimaeus received his sight and followed Jesus along the road.

335. WAITING IN A TREE

Luke 19

Farther down the road, more people waited for Jesus. The crowd was so big that it was hard to see him easily.

A man named Zacchaeus, who was rather short, decided to climb up in a tree so that he could see Jesus. The view was good from where he sat. When Jesus passed by, he saw Zacchaeus perched up on a limb and yelled: "Come down here, Zacchaeus. I'm going to stay at your house tonight."

The people were surprised Jesus wanted to spend time with Zacchaeus because he was a tax collector for the Romans. Nobody liked him very much because of his job.

"We can't believe Jesus is staying with this sinner," they said.

But the next day, when Zacchaeus stood before them, he pledged to Jesus that he would give half of everything he had to the poor.

"If I have taken more taxes from a man than I should have," he said. "I will pay him back four times as much as I took."

Everyone marveled that Jesus had caused Zacchaeus to turn from his sinful ways.

336. STONES WILL SHOUT

Luke 19

Before they reached Jerusalem, Jesus told two of his disciples to go into town and find a donkey's young colt. He wanted them to bring it back to him.

"If anyone asks why you are taking the donkey," he said, "tell them that the Lord needs it."

Later the disciples returned with the donkey and spread some of their clothes over the animal's back. Jesus climbed on the little colt.

He rode down the Mount of Olives with his disciples walking beside him. The disciples shouted praise to God loudly so everyone nearby could hear them.

"Blessed is the King who comes to us in the name of the Lord," they said.

Some Pharisees heard the yelling. They said to Jesus, "Tell your disciples to quiet down."

Jesus said to them, "If these men stop shouting praise, the rocks will shout out instead."

337. A ROYAL WELCOME

Luke 19

As Jesus entered the city on the donkey people lined the streets before him. They took off their coats and threw them on the ground to make a path for him. Some of them took palm branches off the trees and waved them in the air.

Jesus cried as he looked down on the city of Jerusalem. He knew there were many people who still did not believe in him. God wanted Jerusalem to be a peaceful place for his chosen people. But they turned away from him again and again.

The people on the streets were filled with glory for all the things they had seen and heard Jesus do. They shouted out praise to him and called him the king of Israel.

The Pharisees were frightened by what they saw. They could tell Jesus was gaining power over the people.

"It seems like the whole world is following him," they said. "Now the people listen to him instead of us."

338. CHEATING IN THE TEMPLE

Luke 19

The first place Jesus went in Jerusalem was the temple. It shocked him to see the place filled with people buying and selling animals. Moneychangers sat at tables, trading with people for special coins used to pay the temple tax. Everywhere people yelled and shouted at each other over the animals' noise.

As Jesus watched he could tell that the sellers and moneychangers were cheating many people. The more he saw, the more angry he became.

Suddenly, Jesus pushed over tables and chairs. He yelled at the people to get their animals out of the temple. He wouldn't let other buyers and sellers come inside.

"This is to be a house of worship and prayer," he said. "You have turned it into a den of thieves."

The people stood quietly listening to Jesus. They knew he was right and were ashamed of what they had done.

339. MESSAGES

Luke 20

Every day a huge crowd gathered at the temple to hear Jesus tell stories and talk about God's kingdom. Jesus knew the Jewish leaders listened to him, so he decided to tell a parable. It told what was going to happen to the leaders who wanted to destroy him.

"A farmer grew grapes on a big piece of land called a vineyard," Jesus said. "He rented the vineyard to some men to take care of because he had to leave the country for many days.

"At harvest time, the farmers sent a servant to the vineyard. He ordered the servants to collect fruit the men were paying him in rent. But the men were very greedy. They didn't want to pay the farmer, so they killed the servant.

"Then the farmer decided to send his son. Surely, the men would not harm him! But when the son arrived at the vineyard, they killed him, too.

"What will the farmer do to these evil men?" Jesus asked. "He will have them killed and give the land to another group of farmers who are not so greedy and evil."

340. GIVING GOD HIS DUE

Mark 12

The Jewish priests were in the temple when Jesus chased out the thieves. They saw how the people paid attention to everything Jesus told them. Also, they knew Jesus gained more power every day. Somehow the priests needed to have a plot that would get rid of Jesus.

The religious leaders sent several Pharisees to meet with Jesus. They wanted to see if they could trick Jesus into saying something against the Roman government.

"Is it right for us to pay taxes to Caesar and the Romans?" they asked.

Jesus knew the Pharisees were trying to trick him. If he said no, they would have him arrested. And if he said yes, the people would be angry with him.

"Bring me a coin," he said.

They gave him one, and he asked the leaders whose picture was on it. When they answered Caesar's, he said to them. "Then we must give Caesar what belongs to Caesar, and give God what belongs to God."

341. LIGHTING THE LAMPS

Matthew 25

Jesus wanted the people to be ready to enter his kingdom when they died. He told the crowds many stories of how important it was to follow him when he called them.

"Ten young women took their lamps and went to meet the bridegroom at a wedding. Five of them acted foolishly. They didn't take extra oil for the lamps in case they had to wait a long time. The other five were wise. They brought plenty of extra oil.

"They all fell asleep as they waited, and suddenly someone yelled at them to come meet the bridegroom. It was the middle of the night. The five young women who did not bring oil found that their lamps went out. They could not see in the dark room.

"The five wise ones told the foolish ones to buy more oil because they didn't have enough to share. When the foolish ones returned, the door was locked. The doorman turned them away from the feast."

Jesus said that people must always be prepared to meet him, because they could not know when he might come for them.

342. DIVIDING THE FLOCK

Matthew 25

Jesus wanted the disciples to know what would happen when he came back to judge the earth. He said he would be like a shepherd who divides his flocks, putting the sheep on his right side and the goats on his left.

Jesus told them, "I will tell the sheep on the right to come up to the kingdom they inherited from my Father, who has prepared it for them.

"'When I was hungry and thirsty, you gave me food and water,' I will say to them. 'When I needed clothing and shelter, you gave them to me.' The righteous will say, 'When did we do these things?' And I will answer, 'Just as you did these things for others, you did them for me.'

"But I will say to the people on the left that I came to them also—yet they did not give me food and water. They will ask when I came to them. I will say that every time one of my followers came to them it was me. By turning their backs on my people, they turned their backs on me.

"Then they will be sent away to be punished, while my 'sheep' will have eternal life."

343. JUDAS SELLS OUT

Matthew 26

Judas Iscariot was one of Jesus' disciples. He was not as loyal and faithful as the others. He still believed in his heart that money was the most important thing on earth.

When Lazarus's sister, Mary, poured expensive perfume on Jesus' feet, it made Judas very angry. He told Jesus they should sell the perfume to get money for the poor. But since Judas took care of the money, he thought he could put some aside for himself.

Judas knew the Jewish priests and Pharisees wanted to lay a trap for Jesus. He figured they would pay a high price to get their hands on him. So he went to the priests at night and asked what they would pay to have Jesus brought to them.

"We will give you thirty pieces of silver," the priests said.

That was a lot of money, so Judas planned how he could turn over Jesus to the priests.

344. A ROOM FOR THE FEAST

Matthew 26

It was time for the disciples to prepare the meal they would serve for the Passover Feast. "Where will we have our Passover meal?" the disciples asked Jesus.

"Go into the city and look for a man carrying a pitcher of water," he said. "Follow him back to the house and ask to see the owner. Ask him which room the Master will use during the Passover meal."

The disciples did as Jesus told them to do. When they found the man's house, he showed them a large room upstairs that was already set up with tables and chairs. They found everything they needed to fix the unleavened bread and other food that was a part of the Passover dinner.

345. THE LAST PASSOVER

Matthew 26

That evening Jesus arrived at the house to celebrate the Passover with his disciples. After they sat down, Jesus said something that disturbed them very much.

"One of you sitting at this table will turn me in to my enemies," he said.

The disciples looked at each other. They couldn't believe one of them would betray Jesus. This made them sad. Later that evening Jesus took the bread that was on the table and broke it into little pieces. "This is my body," he said. "Take it."

Then he passed his cup around the room and told each dis-

When Jesus came back to the place he had left the three disciples, he found them asleep. He was angry with them because they had not stayed awake to keep watch.

349. JESUS IS ARRESTED

John 18

Jesus awakened the disciples. "Get up now," he said. "The person who is betraying me is here."

They saw Judas coming toward them with a group of soldiers and priests from the temple.

"The person I will kiss is the man you want," Judas whispered to the soldiers. Then he walked over to greet Jesus with a kiss.

"Why have you come here?" Jesus asked, even though he knew the answer.

"We're looking for Jesus of Nazareth," one of the soldiers said.

"I am he," Jesus answered.

Peter pulled his sword and cut off the ear of one of the men.

"Put that sword away," Jesus said to him. "This is the way my Father wants it."

Then Jesus said, "Why are you arresting me here like I was a thief? You could have taken me while I was in the temple."

Jesus' disciples were very afraid. They ran away as the soldiers tied up Jesus and took him back to Jerusalem.

350. THE QUESTIONING

Matthew 26

All that night, the priests and religious leaders questioned people, wanting to find someone who had seen Jesus do or say something wrong. Then they could convict Jesus and have him put to death.

One by one, witnesses were brought in, but none of them gave stories that made Jesus look like a criminal.

"I heard him say he could tear down the temple and build it back in three days," said one witness.

"What do you say about that?" the high priest asked Jesus.

Jesus said nothing.

"Are you or are you not Christ, the Son of God?" the priests yelled.

"I am," Jesus said. "Soon you will see me sitting at the right hand of God."

"Did you hear that?" the priest shouted. "What more proof do we need? This man actually thinks he is the Son of God!"

Everyone began to yell that Jesus should be crucified. They spit at him. The servants covered his face so he could not see.

351. THE SUNRISE

Mark 14

Peter followed the soldiers to find out where they were taking Jesus.

While he watched, the men took Jesus inside the home of a priest. Peter walked over to where some servants were sitting and warmed himself by the fire.

One of the priest's maids came outside and saw Peter.

"Did you come with that man, Jesus?" she asked.

Peter acted like he didn't know what she was talking about. He feared the soldiers might take him prisoner, too, if they found out he was a disciple.

He went out on the porch and heard a rooster crowing in the distance. Then he looked over and saw the maid talking to a soldier. She was pointing at Peter.

"I was not with that man," Peter said. Just then he heard the rooster crow again.

"Are you sure?" asked the maid.

"Yes, I'm sure," Peter answered.

Peter heard the rooster crow a third time and saw the sun rising in the sky. Then he remembered that Jesus had said Peter would deny him. Peter began to cry.

352. A BIG MISTAKE

Matthew 27

After the priests paid Judas thirty pieces of silver, they left Judas alone to think about what he had done. Although he was now a rich man, Judas was not happy about how he had gotten his money.

The morning after Jesus was taken prisoner, Judas learned that the priests were planning to have Jesus killed. He felt very badly because he had not wanted Jesus to be harmed. Maybe if he returned the money to the priests they would let Jesus go.

Judas took the silver and ran back to the temple.

"I have made a big mistake," Judas said to the priests. "I have turned in an innocent man."

"Who cares what you think?" they said.

So Judas dropped the money on the table and left. Later the priests discovered Judas had hanged himself. They knew then they could not keep the money Judas left them.

They used the silver to buy a piece of land where strangers could be buried. People called it the field of blood, because Judas died for it.

353. THE TRIAL

Luke 23

Once the Jewish priests and religious leaders decided Jesus was guilty, they took him into Jerusalem to stand trial before the Roman governor, Pontius Pilate.

"This man refused to pay his taxes," they said. "He claims he is Christ the King."

"Do you claim to be king of the Jews?" Pilate asked Jesus.

"So you say," Jesus told him.

Pilate did not think Jesus had committed any crime. He wanted to let Jesus go, but the leaders did not agree. Pilate learned Jesus was from Galilee, so he sent him to Herod who was also in Jerusalem.

Herod questioned Jesus for a long time. He wanted Jesus to perform a miracle. But when Jesus refused to speak to him, Herod made fun of Jesus.

Meanwhile, Pilate told the chief priests and rulers that neither he nor Herod found Jesus guilty of a crime. "What shall we do with him?" he asked.

354. BARABBAS SET FREE

Luke 23

The people answered Pilate's question about what to do with Jesus. They wanted him killed. But Pilate knew that because it was Passover, he could let one prisoner go free.

"I am letting Jesus go. He has done nothing that he should be put to death for," Pilate said.

"Do away with him" the people yelled. "Free Barabbas!"

Barabbas was another prisoner being held on a murder charge.

"But if I give you Barabbas, what will I do with Jesus?" Pilate asked.

"Crucify him! Crucify him!" the people shouted.

What the people said saddened Pilate. His wife told him she had dreamed about Jesus and that he was innocent. Pilate believed this, also. Still, he had to do what the people wanted or else they might start a riot in protest. He asked that a bowl of water be brought to him. With all the people watching, Pilate rinsed his hands.

"I am washing the innocent blood of Jesus from my hands," he said. "I'll not be responsible for what happens to him now."

355. BEARING THE CROSS

Matthew 27

The soldiers quickly carried out the order given to them. They took Jesus away, stripped off his clothes, and beat him. Then they threw a purple robe over his shoulders. One soldier twisted a thorny vine into a crown shape and put it on Jesus' head.

"Hail to the king of the Jews!" they shouted.

Some took reeds and hit Jesus' head. They kneeled down before him, spitting on him while others stood by and laughed.

Once they finished with their cruel jokes, the soldiers pulled the robe away and gave Jesus back his clothes. They brought out the wooden cross on which Jesus would be crucified. Jesus was too weak to carry the cross himself, so they made a man traveling on the road carry it for him.

The man's name was Simon. He was a Jew from another country. Simon walked with the group, carrying Jesus' cross up to a place called Golgotha, or "place of the skull."

356. JESUS IS CRUCIFIED

Mark 15

When they reached the place where Jesus would be crucified, the soldiers laid Jesus on the cross and nailed his hands and feet onto the wood. Then they raised up the cross in the air and struck its bottom end into the ground.

They put a sign on the cross that said, "The King of the Jews." Beneath the cross, Jesus' mother, Mary, and a few other people gathered to mourn Jesus. They watched in horror as the soldiers drew names to see who would get Jesus' coat.

Two other men were crucified the same day. Their crosses stood on either side of Jesus.

"If you really are Christ, why don't you save yourself and us, too?" one of them asked.

"Don't you think you should have a little more respect for God?" said the other one. "You and I are condemned to die, but we deserve it. This man has done nothing." Then he asked Jesus to remember him in heaven. Jesus said that he would see him there that very day.

357. A DARK DAY

Mark 15

Jesus looked down at the soldiers who caused him so much pain. He had every reason to be angry with them, but Jesus taught that people must forgive one another.

"Forgive them, Father," he said. "They don't know what they are doing."

Then Jesus saw his mother Mary standing next to the disciple, John. He told them to look after each other like mother and son from then on.

A great darkness fell over the land. Jesus could no longer take the terrible pain he was suffering. He looked up to heaven and said, "My God, why have you turned away from me?"

Jesus asked for water. Someone put a sponge filled with old wine vinegar up to Jesus' lips and he tasted the wine. "It is finished," he said. Jesus bowed his head and died.

Even though it was still early in the day, the sun disappeared from view, and the ground shook in a powerful earthquake. The people became very frightened. "He must have really been the Son of God," they said.

358. JESUS' TOMB

Luke 23

Jesus died on Friday, the day before the sabbath. The soldiers wanted to bury Jesus' body quickly, so they could take up the crosses before the sabbath. They went around to the bodies of Jesus and the other two men, making sure they were dead.

Sometimes the soldiers broke the prisoners' legs to see if they were still alive, but they left Jesus' legs alone.

Joseph, one of Jesus' followers, heard about Jesus' death and went to see Pilate. He wanted to donate a tomb he owned, so Jesus could have a proper burial. Pilate agreed Joseph could take Jesus' body.

So Joseph and Nicodemus, another of Jesus' followers, took Jesus to the tomb and wrapped his body in linen cloth. They sprinkled his body with spices as the Jewish laws said, but they did not have all the oils they needed. Mary and some other women who had come with them said they would bring the oils back after the sabbath.

Then the two men rolled a huge stone in front of the tomb to seal it off. As she watched these things, Mary was very sad.

359. JESUS IS ALIVE!

Matthew 28

Two guards were assigned to guard the tomb. Early on Sunday morning, they felt the ground rumble, and watched as the stone in front of the tomb rolled away. They fainted because they were so scared.

Shortly after that, Mary and a friend of Jesus' named Mary Magadalene came to the tomb bringing oils and spices for Jesus' body. They were shocked to see that the rock had moved. The women rushed inside to see what had happened to Jesus' body.

An angel greeted them as they walked inside. The women were very frightened and fell to their knees.

"You have come looking for Jesus of Nazareth," the angel said. "He is not here. He has risen from death."

The women looked at the place where Jesus' body had been. It was empty.

"Go back and tell Jesus' disciples the wonderful news," the angel said. "Tell them Jesus will meet them in Galilee."

360. COME AND SEE

Luke 24

Mary and Mary Magdalene were amazed by what they saw and heard. Suddenly, they saw Jesus himself standing in front of them. The women wanted to touch him, but he told them they must not.

"Go tell my disciples that you have seen me and that I am going up to meet my Father," Jesus said.

Mary Magdalene ran to find the disciples. Mary hurried after her. They told the disciples everything that had happened. None of the disciples believed what the women said. But Peter was curious, so he went back and found the empty tomb. He began to wonder what was going on.

One day, two disciples were walking down the road on their way to Emmaus. A man walked up to them and asked why they were so sad. They told him that their leader and beloved friend, Jesus, had been cruelly put to death.

"Isn't that what the prophets told us would happen in the Scriptures?" the man said.

Then he began to talk about the Scriptures from Moses on down. The disciples were fascinated. They invited the man to dinner, so they could talk more.

361. DINNER GUEST

Luke 24

When the men got home, they sat down to a meal of meat and bread. One of them passed the bread to their guest. The man took the bread, blessed it, and gave a piece of it to each of them. As they took the bread, they realized their dinner guest was really Jesus himself!

They looked up, but Jesus had disappeared from sight. The two men ran to find the other disciples in Jerusalem. When they found them, one man told the disciples what happened.

"Jesus has risen just like we were told," he said. "Peter saw him, too."

They told the others how the stranger broke bread like Jesus used to do. Then at that moment, Jesus appeared to them.

"Peace be with you," he said.

Jesus told them not to be frightened. He showed them the scars on his hands and feet to prove he was really Christ.

362. DOUBTING THOMAS

John 20

The disciple named Thomas had not been with the other disciples when Jesus appeared to them. When he returned from his trip, the disciples were eager to tell Thomas the wonderful news.

"We have seen Jesus!" they said.

Thomas thought they were playing some kind of bad joke on him.

"Unless I see the scars on his hands for myself, I won't believe you," he said.

Another week went by, and the disciples were sitting in their house. They looked up to see Jesus standing before them.

"Peace be with you," he said. He walked over to Thomas and said, "Touch my hands and feel the scars I have from the nails and the cross. I want you to believe in me."

Thomas was amazed.

"My Lord, it is you," he said.

"You believe me now because you have seen me," Jesus said. "I will bless those who believe in me and yet have not seen me."

363. A BIG CATCH

John 21

The disciples had gone out on their boat and fished through the night without catching a thing. The next morning they started back for the shore.

"Catch anything?" a man yelled to them from the land.

They yelled back that they hadn't caught any fish.

"Throw your net over the right side of the boat," the man told them. When they did, the net filled up with so many fish, it could barely hold them all.

"It's Jesus!" Peter shouted. He jumped over the side of the boat and waded to shore.

By the time the other disciples arrived, Jesus had started a fire.

"Bring me the fish you caught," he said.

After they ate, Jesus took Peter away from the group. He asked Peter if he loved him, and Peter said he did.

"Then feed my sheep for me when I'm gone," he said.

Peter knew Jesus meant for him to keep on teaching the lessons Jesus had taught all his followers.

364. RISING TO HEAVEN

Acts 1

The last time that Jesus spoke to his disciples, he told them to wait in Jerusalem for a special visitor.

"John the Baptist baptized with water," he said. "But you will be baptized with the Holy Spirit." The Holy Spirit would give the disciples power to do many good works and miracles just as Jesus had done.

Some of Jesus' followers who were with the disciples asked Jesus when he would come back to lead his kingdom on earth. They wanted to know when he would become the king they hoped for.

"It's not for you to know such things," he said. "Only God knows when that will happen.

After Jesus finished speaking to them, they watched as he rose up into heaven, out of their sight. Two angels appeared next to them."

"Why are you standing here, looking up at the clouds?" the angels asked. "This Jesus you have just watched go up into heaven will come back down to earth the same way someday."

365. THE HOLY SPIRIT

Acts 1 - 2

The disciples met with other followers of Jesus. They prayed together and waited for the Holy Spirit to come.

One day, they heard a rush of wind come through the house where they were sitting. The disciples felt the Holy Spirit entering their bodies. They began to speak in many different languages at the same time.

Other Jews living in the house came running to see what the noise was about. They were amazed to find the disciples speaking in so many different tongues.

"What's happened to these men?" they asked.

Some people thought the disciples had been drinking wine, but Peter told them that was not true. He told them the Holy Spirit had come to them as Jesus had said it would and as the prophets had predicted. Peter preached to them about Jesus and the wonderful things he had done.

The people felt badly about what they had done to Jesus. They asked God to forgive them, and three thousand of them were baptized. They went out to set up a new church for all the people who believed in Christ Jesus.